November 22, 2016

Dear Jim,
    Thank you for your belief in this project and your clever Foreword. I think of you and Helen so often.

Warmly,
Jeanne

Overture

to

Practical Theology

OVERTURE to PRACTICAL THEOLOGY

The Music of Religious Inquiry

Jeanne Stevenson-Moessner

Foreword by James N. Lapsley

CASCADE *Books* • Eugene, Oregon

OVERTURE TO PRACTICAL THEOLOGY
The Music of Religious Inquiry

Cascade Books
An Imprint of Wipf and Stock Publishers
199 W. 8th Ave., Suite 3
Eugene, OR 97401

www.wipfandstock.com

PAPERBACK ISBN: 978-1-4982-8302-1
HARDCOVER ISBN: 978-1-4982-8304-5
EBOOK ISBN: 978-1-4982-8303-8

Cataloguing-in-Publication data:

Names: Stevenson-Moessner, Jeanne. | Lapsley, James N.

Title: Overture to practical theology : the music of religious inquiry , 2nd ed. / Jeanne Stevenson-Moessner ; foreword by James N. Lapsley.

Description: Eugene, OR: Cascade Books, 2016. | Includes bibliographic references and index.

Identifiers: 978-1-4982-8302-1 (paperback) | 978-1-4982-8304-5 (hardcover) | 978-1-4982-8303-8 (ebook)

Subjects: LCSH: Theology, Practical.

Classification: BV3 M64 2016 (print) | BV3 (ebook).

Manufactured in the U.S.A.   11/09/16

To my son, the artist, David Stevenson-Moessner.
The music of his life still lingers.

Contents

Foreword

In her *Overture to Practical Theology*, Jeanne Stevenson-Moessner has taken a new route to introduce seminary students and others to the field of practical theology. Although she is certainly aware of the relatively recent efforts to show the academic credentials of practical theology through careful definition (citing that of David Tracy), analysis of components, and linkages to other disciplines within and without the overall framework of theology, she proceeds by means of a double analogy rather than academic precision to illumine practical theology. Case studies, both actual and fictional also helpfully elucidate aspects of her work.

The first analogy, that of a tree whose roots are in traditional theological disciplines (philosophical theology according to Friedrich Schleiermacher, the "Father" of modern theology and the originator of the "tree" analogy), whose trunk is historical theology, and whose branches are practical theology, emphasizes the derivative, but also "crown" like, character of practical theology. Practical theology's additional crucial role is in nourishing the other branches of theology through its contact with the environment. This organic analogy serves her well, visually.

The second analogy is that of an orchestra in concert, which emphasizes the connectedness of practical theology to other theological disciplines, rather than as a soloist, or even a kind of "guest soloist," as some writers have regarded it in the past. This analogy obviously is an auditory one, in which the sounds of the orchestra must harmonize and complement one another. Reflecting this analogy, the book is divided into stanzas, rather than chapters.

Stevenson-Moessner is, however, aware that the sounds are not always harmonious. At one point, she explicitly acknowledges that the role of the minister, as conductor, must allow for flexibility which may result in cacophony. "However," she states, "Cacophony precedes harmony and creation." She also devotes a "stanza" to "Discordant Notes." Nevertheless, within this realistic "messiness" (my term, not hers) of parish life, she discerns the possibilities for harmonious and constructive Christian living. These possibilities are the goals of practical theology.

She devotes considerable space to the voices of "post-colonialism." Although I have no intrinsic objection to this term, currently in use among pastoral theologians, I am not sure that it is better understood by all than some of its predecessors with similar meaning—such as anti-authoritarian, non-hierarchical, or even democratic.

I heartily recommend this new work and its analogies to all who would gain a clearer picture and "sound" of the nature of practical theology, even though efforts toward greater conceptual clarity in relation to practice should also continue. I have long entertained doubts that practical theology is susceptible to complete conceptual clarity, so let the tree grow and the orchestra play on.

James N. Lapsley
Hightstown, New Jersey
June 20, 2016

Preface

Practical theology is the music of religious inquiry. Like any discipline in the academy, it involves the rigors of the mind. For years, pastoral theology, a subdiscipline of Practical Theology, has spoken of persons as living human documents in the sense that knowledge and insight flows from persons. Surely knowledge is also attained from written documents and external oral communication. However, the shift in the 1980s to the term "living human document" placed agency within the individual. In this text, a further shift will be made to "living human instruments" which emphasizes not only agency but creativity within persons; practical theology creates a space where living human instruments can be heard, as soloists or in concert. Practical theology is the creative energy of God activated within God's living human instruments. I am using the imagery of music, a universal language, to develop this thesis.

Perhaps I could have used the imagery of ballet for this book since I danced four and a half years with the Memphis Civic Ballet. The smell of resin, the nervousness at curtain call, the sense of envelopment in an artistic endeavor greater than the sum of its parts and players—all of this returns to me as quickly as a breath. However, my purpose in writing this introductory book was better achieved with the imagery of musical orchestration and performance. Therefore, I begin a conversation with you that I have titled an "overture." This "overture" is an exposure to the major themes or movements in practical theology, movements which stand in

relationship to Biblical studies, church history, ethics, social justice, and other disciplines in theology.

Some of the material for this "overture" came unexpectedly
from students in my first semester of teaching at Perkins School
of Theology, fall of 2005. As new faculty, I inherited a course titled
"Issues in Practical Theology" from a professor who was on leave.
In the midst of a geographical move, I was not eager to design
a new syllabus and orchestrate a class that had not been in my
repertoire.

This is background to the class "composition" that unfolded.
Twenty-nine students brought in remarkable, actual cases that
were discussed toward the end of the semester. All cases were an
attempt to get at that elusive query: what is practical theology?
Marcel Viau refers to practical theology's unconfirmed academic
status.[1] Don Browning has aptly summarized another reaction to
an effort to conceptualize an answer:

> The field of practical theology has been throughout its
> history the most beleaguered and despised of the theo-
> logical disciplines. The discipline of theology has had few
> friends even in the church. To admit in academic circles
> that one is a theologian has been, in recent years, to court
> embarrassment. To admit that one is a practical theolo-
> gian invites even deeper skepticism. To admit in a major
> university that one is a practical theologian has been to
> invite humiliation.[2]

Although I had a different experience of practical theology
while I completed my doctor of theology at the University of Basel, Switzerland, I do agree with Don Browning's assessment of the
necessity of practical theology's interaction with and respect from
other disciplines. Leading the street procession at the beginning of
each academic year in Basel, a day called the Day of Academics, or
Dies Academicus, are the practical theologians followed by those in
New Testament, Old Testament, church history, and systematics or
dogmatics. Practical theology was anything but an embarrassment.

1. Viau, *Practical Theology*, xi.
2. Browning, *A Fundamental Practical Theology*, 3.

Upon returning to the United States in the 1980s, I witnessed the isolation of practical theology as Browning observed.

Theologians, like artists, are given the opportunity to be embraced in an endeavor greater than the sum of our fields. We are capable of creating a rhythm that can be organically and structurally related to other theological disciplines and to other fields in academic research. I am assuming *a priori* that we are connected to those doing ministry.

The International Academy of Practical Theology and the American Association of Practical Theology have made great strides to foster this interaction with other disciplines.[3] Other organizations such as the Society for Pastoral Theology encourage interaffiliations.[4] It is through the work of pastoral theologians that I began to understand how an individual might be described in relationship to others. The founders of the Clinical Pastoral Education (CPE) movement, such as Anton Boisen, began to view the individual as "a living human document," not a passive receptacle.[5] Granted, a written book is instructive and imparts knowledge. However, an individual also grants wisdom and offers reflective insight as a living document. As much, if not more, is learned by listening to, by "reading," and by receiving narrative from a person as from absorbing inscribed verbiage and vocabulary. The CPE movement began to focus on the interaction between the CPE resident and the patient and on the resident's reconstruction through verbatims of what the patient revealed. This shift in methodology was significant; the patients and the residents became the most valuable textbooks. A number of theologians developed

3. Don S. Browning, Riet Bons-Storm, Richard Osmer, Friedrich Schweitzer, James Fowler, Karl Ernst Nipkow, Dietrich Roessler, and Hans Van Der Ven were founders of the International Academy of Practical Theology, an organization that has increased worldwide visibility and credibility in the field.

4. The Society for Pastoral Theology is an academic forum for pastoral theologians. According to the late Liston Mills, the Society for Pastoral Theology was "conceived" in the Philadelphia airport in the late 1970s during a conversation between the two pastoral theologians, Mills and Jim Lapsley. See preface to Childs and Waanders, *The Treasure of Earthen Vessels,* ix.

5. Gerkin, *The Living Human Document,* 30.

the concept of "the living human document," but I learned more about this novel way of looking at persons from Charles Gerkin. It was my windfall to study with him at Georgia Baptist Hospital in Atlanta, Georgia, in a clinical residency in pastoral care and counseling. Other theologians have introduced equally compelling images, among them that of "the living human web."[6] What I am offering in addition to these prevalent images is that of the person as "living human instrument" designated to give voice or sound uniquely but also created to be in concert with others. My presentation is not too far removed from the Stone Center's work on "self-in-relationship" or "self-in-relation." Both "word paintings," or figures of speech, place emphasis on individuality and on relatedness. Both individuality and connectedness are needed for individual growth and that of theological education. What is practical theology? It is the creative energy of God activated within God's living human instruments. As such, it becomes the music of religious inquiry, whether formalized in the academy as a discipline or exercised in the world.

An Overture to Practical Theology differs in three ways from my earlier work (*Prelude to Practical Theology,* Abingdon). Comparable to the approach of Elizabeth Moltmann-Wendel who theologizes from the perspective of violated bodies, I test theology now from the position of suffering; for me, it is that profound shattering that comes with the loss of a child. The last entry, a Requiem, follows the death of my 26-year-old son, David. Personally, what I write must be tested against the last entry. Secondly, I write with an emphasis on interconnectedness in theological education; to do so, I resurrect a discarded image from the early works of Friedrich Schleiermacher. I am not trying to mix images, rather I am using an earlier contribution from Schleiermacher to show the interrelationship of Practical Theology with other academic disciplines. The image of a tree with roots, branches, and foliage illustrates circular and cyclical movement which can occur among

6. Miller-McLemore, "The Living Human Web," in *Through the Eyes of Women,* 9–26. See also Miller-McLemore, "The Living Human Web," in *Images of Pastoral Care,* 40–46.

theological disciplines in the academy, Thirdly, an overture to practical theology must include not only the strains of social justice but the cacophony of political risk and involvement.

I proceed with indebtedness to those like the late Chuck Gerkin and the active Bonnie Miller-McLemore, who, together with others, have offered a full program of conceptual repertoire. I trust that my work will add to theirs and others in the field, some of whom are in the annotated bibliography. I hope that our work will contribute to collegial, noncompetitive interaction with other disciplines. To admit we are practical theologians in academe is to invite interassociation.

I must confess that I, along with other young ballet dancers in the Memphis Civic Ballet, often dreamed of being the prima ballerina, or lead dancer. Surely, we lived in the hope of being a soloist. It is a normal fancy. I have also alluded to the fact that, on the night of any given performance, when the toe shoes were tied securely, when the lights were lowered, when the audience hushed, and when the opening bars of music rose from the orchestra pit, I was enraptured by the sublimity of corporate creativity. It did not matter that I was in the chorus, at least not for the two or three hours of the performance. I was a lover of a beauty that was greater than the individual parts.

Such ravishment I have seen when a healthy baby is born, when debts are cancelled, when vows are taken, when a sacrament transcends the moment. I ask you to read on as an aesthete, as a living human instrument—uniquely created. I hope you will find connection. If your foot is bobbing and your toes are tapping, you are hearing the warm-up to an overture in practical theology. Dim the lights!

Jeanne Stevenson-Moessner, Dr.Theol.
Perkins School of Theology,
SMU Dallas, Texas
August 2016

Acknowledgments

There are a number of people who need to take a bow or to curtsy. I thank my students at Perkins School of Theology at Southern Methodist University for their response to my orchestration of the class, "Issues in Practical Theology," in the fall of 2005. Several of them have provided material and insight through case studies to answer the question: what is practical theology anyway? These students were both an active audience and orchestra.

I am grateful for the backup of my family, especially my husband, David Moessner. Our marriage is a wonderful duet. Jean Moessner, our daughter, inspired the artwork in Stanza One; David Moessner, our son, exposed us to contemporary forms of music and art; Jean Stevenson, my mother, Bob and Cleo Stevenson, my brothers, have been backers and supporters of my work as well. Following the death of our son, Vanessa Sims wrote the poem "To Mom" and graciously gave permission for its inclusion. Applause also goes to the behind-the-scenes crew: Dr. Martha Robbins, the Rev. Dr. Susan Sharpe, Sara Staley, Dr. Harry and Linda Moessner, Blanche Montesi, Mary Leah Friedline, Dr. Evon Flesberg, Dr. Kathy Armistead, Martha Lynn Ayres, Vic and Bill Ayres, Leon Hammond, Ellen Klyce, Claire McCaskill Hughes, Rev. Mary Stewart Hall, the Rev. Amy Williams Fowler, Nancy McLemore, Connie Nelson, Dr. Beka Miles, Dr. Mark Stamm, Dr. Rick Rosengarten, Dr. Margaret Mitchell, Linda and Dale Wlochal, the Gills from Nashville, Elizabeth Stevenson, the Moessner family, St. Mary's class of 1966, our friends from Nativity Church,

Acknowledgments

Katherine Flahive, Dr. Felicity Kelcourse, Dr. Pat Davis, Dr. Carol Adams, and all my colleagues and students at Perkins School of Theology who supported us in our loss of David.

In closing, I want to turn the spotlight on David Stevenson Moessner, a man with a strong and passionate heart. The last year of his life was filled with a grace and love that overcame many obstacles. The music of his life embraced us all.

STANZA 1

Warming Up

Practical Theology-in-Relationship

INTRODUCTION

An orchestra consists of musicians in relationship. This connectedness results in sonatas, concertos, symphonies, and requiems that are distinct from a solo performance. Theology is the music of religious inquiry. Theology is also the formal study of faith, doctrine, history, religious education, sacred texts, and spirituality. Theologians, like musicians, are given the opportunity to create beyond the formal disciplines in which they have been trained. In community, they create a religious rhythm that can be organically and structurally related to others in ministry, in theological investigation, in academic research.

This book will look at one discipline, or area, of theology: practical theology. Instead of regarding practical theology as a "soloist" or "guest musician," this book will consider how practical theology plays in concert with other disciplines or areas in theology. As the discussion "warms up," Stanza One presents practical theology-in-relationship to other theological disciplines using an image that I found in the early works of German theologian Friedrich Schleiermacher. It is an organic image that has much potential for theology. Unfortunately, Schleiermacher discarded the image after it was severely criticized. He failed to underscore the circular and revitalizing movement among the areas of theological inquiry that he aptly depicted in his "scandalous" model. The model that occasioned such a strong reaction was that of a tree:

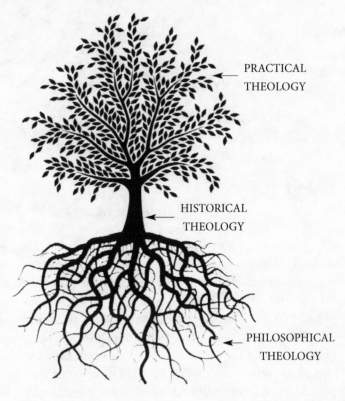

PRACTICAL
THEOLOGY

HISTORICAL
THEOLOGY

PHILOSOPHICAL
THEOLOGY

The vertical thrust of the tree, of course, placed practical theology at the top as the crown, or highest part, of the structure. The "scandal" of this image grew out of the hierarchical interpretation of the tree analogy in which the sap or "living substance of reflection" flowed only upward, from the roots to the crown. Contemporary theologians have noted other examples of Schleiermacher's "hierarchical thinking."[1] I do not know whether Schleiermacher intended such an inference of superiority with his positioning of practical theology at the top of the tree. I do know that the "hierarchical representation" of the crown as the highest point of theological reflection neglected both the equality and mutuality of all three parts of the tree as well as the circular pattern of movement among the various parts, including the earth. The branches, the foliage, the fruits, the leaves, and the flowers all continue to fall and to flow to the ground to replenish the soil from which the roots and trunk grow. Leonardo Boff, in *Cry of the Earth, Cry of the Poor*, has stated the cycle of enrichment in a similar but unique way: "The forest remains lush because the chain of nutrients is closed. Materials are decomposing on the soil, its covering, which is composed of leaves, fruits, small roots, and animal excrement. These things are enriched by the water dripping from the leaves and running off the trunks. It is not the soil that nourishes the leaves, but rather the trees that nourish the soil."[2]

Thus, "the crown" can be interpreted nonhierarchically as the upper extremity that is connected organically to the whole. It is also expansive to note that some trees like older banyan trees have aerial prop roots. The European Beech has aerial roots as do swamp mangroves and certain rainforest trees in New Zealand. Branches can also extend to the ground as in the weeping cherry, fig, and willow trees. In the following pages, I will reclaim and recycle this organic image of the tree because of the unexplored possibilities it has yet to offer.

1. Rieger, "Friedrich Schleiermacher," 274–76. Hierarchical thinking is attributed to Schleiermacher's comparison of different tribes in Australia and Africa, his depiction of gradations of life and stages of development, and his Christology.

2. Boff, *Cry of the Earth, Cry of the Poor*, 90.

BACKGROUND

In 1946, while theologian Karl Barth was spending the summer semester at the University of Bonn, he found in the rubble and ruins of war a bust of theologian Friedrich Schleiermacher. In some ways, it may seem that I am doing the same in this book—lifting an old image of Schleiermacher's writings out of the remains of theological forays. These contemporary forays or discussions often delve into the much-discussed "clerical paradigm" attributed to Schleiermacher. The "clerical paradigm" grew out of a German context in the nineteenth century that envisioned the pastor or cleric as the "product" of the five-year, rigorous course of theological study. This, a controversial assessment, will be explored later in this chapter.

Authors such as Keith Clements suggest that feminist theology, with its emphasis on interconnectedness, could well offer additional insights on the images offered by Friedrich Schleiermacher.[3] This suggestion follows mention of the startling admission that Schleiermacher made to Charlotte von Kathen: "If ever I find myself sportively indulging in an impossible wish, it is, that I were a woman."[4] According to one editor of his works, "this confession has provoked wry smiles or raised eyebrows from later commentators who are inclined to commend Schleiermacher to a psychiatrist without further ado."[5] Nevertheless, as a feminist theologian interested in healthy interdependency, I have chosen to delve into this discarded image, that is, Schleiermacher's tree of theology, an image critiqued by others. He later discarded the image in the second edition of the Brief Outline of the Study of Theology (Kurze Darstellung des theologischen Studiums), a change which occurred during the time of his lectures in Halle and Berlin.

In this chapter, I am assuming, first, that there is something that beckons persons into connectedness. Every embryo begins in relationship in utero. After birth, infants thrive on the beam

---

3. Clements, Friedrich Schleiermacher, 22.

4. Schleiermacher, The Life of Schleiermacher, 382.

5. Clements, Friedrich Schleiermacher, 22.

or gleam in the eyes of the beholders and caretakers. As normal development moves into self differentiation, there is a concurrent need for healthy relationship to others. Second, I am working on the additional assumption that, underlying our endeavors of self-differentiation in denominations, disciplines, and guilds, we are created to be organically related to others in ministry and theology. By *organically*, I mean more than having systemic coordination as a conductor would coordinate or assemble an orchestra. *Organic* is, according to Webster's, "possessed of complex structure comparable to that of living beings." This concept is not so far removed from the Hebrew Bible's portrayal of creation through narratives that portray people as descendants of Adam and Eve. We are the family of humankind or the family of faith. Third, I am assuming that practical theology is an interdisciplinary enterprise and as such, is also interrelated with other theological disciplines.

With these assumptions, I have been drawn to reconsider Schleiermacher's image of the organic unity of the theological disciplines in his *Brief Outline* of 1811, the image of the "tree" of theology. Finding an original copy of the *Brief Outline* of 1811 (*Kurze Darstellung des theologischen Studiums zum Behuf einleitender Vorlesungen*) in Tübingen, Germany, I reexamined this image. Such a sense of organic unity is not to be taken for granted in theological education. Without such an articulation of the interplay and interdependence among the disciplines, what theological institutions like seminaries and divinity schools offer will be at best a creative collection and combination of courses.

Schleiermacher reorganized the theological disciplines into three areas of inquiry: philosophical theology, historical theology, and practical theology. Philosophical theology dealt with the essence, the concepts, the first principles, the "idea" of Christianity. Schleiermacher in 1811 wrote: "Philosophical theology is the root of all theology."[6] Thus, the description of the "root" of theology is given. Historical theology, which included biblical studies, church

---

6. "Die philosophische Theologie is *die Wurzel* der gesamten Theologie" (Schleiermacher, *Einleitung*, 26).

history, dogmatic or systematic theology, and church statistics,[7] was an inquiry into the Christian faith community, past and present. "Historical theology is essentially the trunk of theological study and encompasses in its own way the other two parts within itself."[8] Thus, the picture of the body, or trunk, is given to the paradigm. In addition, historical theology includes in its own way both philosophical and practical theology. Practical theology, accordingly, is "the crown of theological study."[9] From these depictions of roots, trunk or body, and crown came the image of the tree, a living organism, illustrative of the organic unity of the three areas of theological inquiry.

Schleiermacher anticipated that the attack on this image would come from his placement of practical theology as the crown. After all, practical theology as a theological science had come under suspicion since G. J. Planck had relegated it to the appendix of his popular encyclopedia in 1795.[10] However, the main attack on his image came from its vertical construct: "the image of a tree implies that the sap, the living substance of reflection, moves from the roots through the trunk to the crown, but never in the other direction."[11] What was missed, of course, in this analysis was the circular movement, from living water in the earth, to sap in the tree, to fruition and flowering among the branches, to the shedding of foliage to replenish the soil. However, we too easily forget the organic unity, the attempt to see the areas of theological inquiry as interdependent, once the image is discarded. Perhaps, we do not see the theological disciplines divided in the threefold way Schleiermacher constructed. Perhaps, there are other criticisms to engage with his image of the organic unity

7. Schleiermacher, *Christian Caring*, 22.

8. "Die historische Theologie ist *der eigentliche Koerper* des gesamten theologischen Studiums und fasst auf ihre Art auch die andern beiden Teile in sich" (*Einleitung*, 36).

9. "Die praktische Theologie ist *die Krone* des theologischen Studiums" (*Einleitung*, 31).

10. Schleiermacher, *Christian Caring*, 21. The term *practical theology* had not even appeared until the seventeenth century.

11. Ibid, 23.

of the disciplines. Perhaps, as a practical theologian, I gravitate to Schleiermacher's image because it offers my discipline a way to be vitally related to the other disciplines from whom my colleagues and I often feel severed. Using Schleiermacher's image, practical theology bears fruit, offers shade for sojourners, provides a nesting place for wayfarers, and connects its branches to other trees as in the Black Forest near Tübingen, Germany. Perhaps, you, like me, will like an image such as this because it appeals to the part of you that expresses itself in images, metaphors, pictures, and symbols. Without some way to articulate our interconnectedness among theological disciplines, what we offer will only be a collection of materials and resources—like piles of hardwood, firewood, pine, or timber—to be constructed and reconstructed as needed.

The Schleiermacheian "clerical paradigm" lures us to look again. In a European environment the theological disciplines can be divided today as follows: biblical studies, dogmatics or systematics, church history, and practical theology. Just as law schools train men and women to exit as lawyers, so theological schools train men and women to function as pastors—and to reflect as theologians. Thus, the much-critiqued "clerical paradigm"[12] in the Schleiermacheian tradition created and creates pastor theologians who enter the parish after five years of theological study (the *Lizentiat*), which involves an examination after two years of study (*Zwischenexam*) and a state exam after the entire five years of study (*Staatsexam*). Preceding this theological training a European student has thirteen years of rigorous high school (*Gymnasium*); only the top students enter high school to begin with, as some less-serious students are channeled into trade schools. Thus, the theological student has had previous exposure to not only the classical disciplines in *Gymnasium* but also numerous languages, including Latin. The five-year course of theological study includes a mandatory intern year (*Vikariat*). When I hear the "clerical paradigm" under attack for turning out clerics, I must remind myself how well-trained the average European pastor is for theological reflection. They have not simply acquired ministerial skills and tech-

12. This phrase was introduced by Edward Farley, *Theologia*, 87.

niques for their ministry. Quite the contrary, the European pastor has been described as *Mann des Nachdenkens*, or as a theologian, concerned with content and proclamation.[13] The American pastor has been described as a pragmatician, *Mann der Tat*. According to one Dutch theologian, Heije Faber, the emphasis on ministry is different. When you ask an American pastor to show you "the church," he or she will show not only the pulpit but also the kitchen, Sunday school rooms, fellowship hall, activity building or family life center, lounge, and so on. In Europe, when asked to conduct a tour of the church, a pastor will show the sanctuary with pulpit, that is, the place of worship. Thus, the emphasis is on teaching and proclamation. The European divinity student graduates from five years of training with a "clericalism" that is profoundly reflective and integrated with all areas in theology

A CASE IN POINT

From a feminist and womanist perspective, practical theology is seen as a discipline-in-relationship.[14] A case study out of a subdiscipline, pastoral theology, illustrates the type of interplay among areas of theological inquiry that creates critical interaction.

One of the founders of the Clinical Pastoral Education Movement, Helen Flanders Dunbar, in her article "Mental Hygiene and Religious Training,"[15] documented a case study of a young man named James Roe, whose image of God contributed to an emotional breakdown. Dunbar, a Yale-trained MD with a PhD in comparative literature from Columbia University and a BD from Union Theological Seminary, with additional work under Anton Boisen, Helene Deutsch, and Carl Gustav Jung, was well prepared to detect the relationship between mental health and religious teachings. In her case study of James Roe, she particularly focused on the portrayal of a suffering God as a model for development.

---

13. Hiltner, "Pastoral Care in Europe and America."

14. Cozad-Neuger, *The Arts of Ministry*.

15. Flanders Dunbar, "Mental Hygiene and Religious Teaching."

Young James was an obedient, passive, only child. At age seven, he lost his father and devoted himself to being good for the sake of his widowed mother who, he thought, had suffered enough in her loss. James's pastor encouraged all these behaviors in the dutiful child. At age fourteen, due to financial misfortunes, he had to support his mother and abandon his plans for education. "The pastor, his constant friend and adviser, talked to him about the discipline of the Cross, and the Christian character that is gained through disappointment."[16] Because of his gentle ways, James became a laughingstock among his peers. At these times, he identified with Christ, the mocked one. James lost one job after another and faced God and the memory of his father with a sense of failure. The pastor continued to speak to him of Christ. Sometime later, in the mental hospital, James told the superintendent that he, James, was Christ.

In this case of James Roe, H. Flanders Dunbar documents the damaging effect of an overarching portrayal of the God of the New Testament as a suffering God. Dunbar challenged teachers of religion to use dynamic symbolism. "Dynamic symbolism points to the infinite and incomprehensible; the use of multiple symbols can prevent an overbearing focus on or concretization of any one of them."[17]

Using the case of James Roe as a springboard to interdisciplinary conversation, I would ask these questions: How do our images of God impact pastoral theology? How do the doctrines of suffering, sin, grace, and atonement play themselves out in this case? What exactly is the New Testament understanding of suffering? For that matter, what was the Hebrew Bible's understanding of suffering as it affected the faithful? Is there no greater love than this, that a [man] lay down his life for his *mother*? What is the discipline of the cross? What is Christian character? What are the ethical issues in this case? How would you critique the pastor's role in the life of James Roe? What is the history of pastoral care in the

16. Ibid, 357.

17. Stevenson-Moessner, "The Psychology of Women and Pastoral Care," 41.

church? Is this case a period piece? If so, what is pastoral care in our moment of history? From a developmental perspective, did James even have a (sense of) self to sacrifice?

The questions engaged by this case study out of the subdiscipline of practical theology demonstrate the potential interconnectedness and organic unity among the modern theological areas: New Testament, Old Testament, systematic theology, church history, and practical theology.

This case activates questions in each discipline. For the practical theologian, the case study helps concretize this interdisciplinary communication. From my viewpoint as a feminist theologian, practical theology-in-relationship to other theological disciplines is a vital concern. The issue has some parallels to a depiction of the individual as a "self-in-relation." This theory posits that we as individuals all begin in-relationship before birth. Much contemporary research out of the Stone Center in Wellesley, Massachusetts, reorganizes developmental theory around this relational context of the person.

It is noteworthy that Schleiermacher not only spoke of the essence of religion as the feeling of dependence but he also lived in intricate interdependence with others.[18] "This side of Schleiermacher's life is not incidental to his theology: his personal relationships with others formed the most pressing and immediate context to his theology, and between his understanding of human friendships and his theology there are the most intimate connections and parallels."[19]

To Henriette Herz, he wrote,

> Ah, dear Jette, be generous and write often to me; that alone can keep me alive for I cannot thrive in solitude. In truth, I am the least independent and least self-sufficing of mortals; indeed, I sometimes doubt whether I be really an individual. I stretch out all my roots and leaves in search of affection; it is necessary for me to feel myself in immediate contact with it, and when I am unable to

18. Clements, *Friedrich Schleiermacher,* 20.

19. Ibid.

drink in full draughts of it, I at once dry up and wither. Such is my nature; there is no remedy for it; and, if there were, I should not wish to employ it.[20]

Whether describing his own relational context or the interrelationship among theological disciplines, Schleiermacher's image of organic unity (roots–trunk–crown) can challenge us to articulate this interplay in our contemporary context.

20. Schleiermacher, *The Life of Schleiermacher,* 20.

STANZA 2

Variations on the Theme
Love of God and Neighbor

INTRODUCTION

In a remote county parish in East Anglia in England, a disfigured and unidentifiable man was found in a recent grave. This was enough cause for the fictitious and idiosyncratic Lord Peter Wimsey to become involved in the case of *The Nine Tailors*, written by Dorothy L. Sayers.[1] In the parish of Fenchurch St. Paul, the heavy rains of a wet summer and fall overwhelmed the sluices and dikes and threatened to cover the land in brackish backwater. The rector, Mr. Venables, began to prepare the ancient church, which had been built on high ground in anticipation of flooding, and he mobilized the community through emergency measures. A disaster team was formed, all documents and valuables were stored in the tower, personal belongings were placed in the nave, animals were corralled in the churchyard in cattle-pens, the Lady chapel

1. Sayers, *The Nine Tailors.*

was allocated for a refreshment room, stores of food were collected and arranged within the church, the well was secured for drinking water, areas of the church were roped off to provide a place for families to sleep, coal was stored for the furnaces, sanitary trenches were dug outside, stoves and copper pots were readied for community soup. The parish church was ready for a thousand villagers. Neighboring parishes stood by to bring additional supplies by boat in the days ahead.

"It was growing dark, and the road was thronged with carts and cattle, hurrying to the safety of Church Hill."[2] In the minutes before the sluice broke and the waters covered the land, Lord Peter Wimsey remarked on the organization within the church:

> Men, women, children, and household goods had been packed into the church. It was nearly seven o'clock and the dusk had fallen. The lamps were lit. Soup and tea were being served in the Lady chapel, babies were crying, the churchyard resounded with the forlorn lowing of cattle and the terrified bleating of sheep. Sides of bacon were being brought in, and thirty wagon-loads of hay and corn were ranged under the church yard. In the only clear space amid the confusion the rector stood behind the walls of the Sanctuary. And over all, the bells tumbled and warned, shouting their alarm across the country.[3]

For fourteen days and nights, the church functioned as a ship in the sea of chaos. Within the church, parishioners conducted daily school while the rector held services. On three evenings a week, concerts and lectures were given. Mrs. Venables presided over sewing parties. Everyone enjoyed the camaraderie at communal meals. Lord Peter Wimsey organized games and drills in the garden. The rector conducted a wedding. A baby was born. The church called Fenchurch St. Paul witnessed among its villagers a variation on the theme: "the increase among [people] of the love of God and neighbor."

2. Ibid, 385.
3. Ibid, 386.

This description of the work of Fenchurch St. Paul is precisely that of theological education. This same "increase" is the conclusion that theologians H. Richard Niebuhr, Daniel Day Williams, and James M. Gustafson reached in their classic study on the purpose of "doing theology." Niebuhr, Williams, and Gustafson visited more than ninety theological seminaries in the 1950s to inquire about the purpose of the church and its ministry. Their results, published in 1956, led them to conclude that the purpose of the church and its ministry is "the increase among [people] of the love of God and neighbor."[4] Restated, the goal or theme is "to continue to seek God's will and vision for our church and community and strive to do all we can to further God's [*basileia*] here on earth."[5]

CASE STUDY

The classroom becomes a lively place for interactive learning when seminarians bring in actual material from the context of their student ministries. In the fall of 2005, every participant in a course titled "Issues in Practical Theology" contributed a *case study*, which is a true situation with the possibility of layers of learning. Usually, a student presents a challenging configuration, one that he or she hopes to better understand. With these grassroots examples, or down-to-earth cases, the sap of theological inquiry flows.

We begin with a case study on evangelism, outreach, education, and discipleship set in Comanche, a rural town of twelve hundred persons; the case calls into question the purpose of the church and ministry. In this small-town context, two of the town's largest businesses have closed, leaving a failed economy in their wake. Many of the stores have closed, and one restaurant serves the entire town. Eighty percent of the town attends church regularly; there are fifteen churches.

This is the story of one church, a small congregation of fifty persons, who offered a "free" meal at the end of each month, in

---

4. Niebuhr, *The Purpose of the Church and Its Ministry.*
5. Dollarhite, "Issues in Practical Theology."

hopes of relating to the community. The objective was to take the Great Commission of Christ (Matt 28:16–20; Matt 25:42–45) and make it come to life in this Oklahoma town. In the words of Pastor Dollarhite, their *theme* was, "How can we be Christ's hands and feet delivering hope to a town that has lost so much hope?"

In their attempts to address this question, the church experienced power struggles between families, conflict over how the food should be prepared, lessons in shared power, attentiveness to the pride of those being served, and the significance of naming the event. Variations on the theme of increasing love of God and neighbor also entailed an awareness of the humbling aspect of receiving a handout and the necessary introspection of those administering the handouts. These perceptions prompted questions of mission, evangelism, pastoral care, and ecclesiology (the nature of the church)—all areas of practical theology.

What is the purpose of the church and its ministry? Perhaps the parish of Fenchurch St.Paul did not reflect in such a focused way as did Pastor Dollarhite's Oklahoma congregation. Yet, the outcome in both churches reflected a working challenge to live into the love of God and neighbor. Here is Pastor Dollarhite's story.

Cacophony in Comanche

Comanche, Oklahoma, had fallen on hard times. Four hundred dollars a month did not stretch enough to cover a family unit, and with the closing of two factories, four hundred dollars was the monthly budget of most Comanche families. During the school year, the majority of schoolchildren could eat free two times daily while at school. Although the town of Comanche was in decline, the school system was continually growing. The Comanche school system served a five-town radius and had a student population of around a thousand students. At least during the academic year, breakfast and lunch were guaranteed for the children in school.

First Church, a congregation of fifty people under Pastor Dollarhite's leadership, was studying two passages in the Gospel of Matthew: 1) an allegory of separating "sheep from goats," the sheep being the followers of Christ, and 2) the passage containing the Great Commission of Christ, which instructed followers to make disciples, to baptize, and to teach.

> For I [Christ as king] was hungry and you gave me nothing to eat, I was thirsty and you gave me nothing to drink, I was a stranger and you did not invite me in, I needed clothes and you did not clothe me, I was sick and in prison and you did not look after me. They [the righteous] also will answer, "Lord, when did we see you hungry or thirsty or a stranger or needing clothes or sick and in prison, and did not help you?" He will reply, "I tell you the truth, whatever you did not do for one of the least of these, you did not do for me." (Matt 25:42–45 NIV)

> Then the eleven disciples went to Galilee, to the mountain where Jesus had told them to go. When they saw him, they worshiped him; but some doubted. Then Jesus came to them and said, "All authority in heaven and in earth has been given to me. Therefore, go and make disciples of all nations, baptizing them in the name of the Father and of the Son and of the Holy Spirit, *and teaching them to obey everything I have commanded you.* And surely I am with you always, to the very end of the age." (Matt 28:16–20 NIV, emphasis added)

The congregation worked on these texts and allowed the texts to work on them. The congregation wondered how to teach both themselves and others an application of the Matthean theme. In their words, "How can a church find Christ in a town that has lost hope?"

Typically in education, teachers realize there are many modes of learning and different types of learners. Some individuals are auditory learners; they learn by hearing. Some are tactile; they learn by constructing, feeling, shaping, and doing with their hands. Some are visual learners; they absorb information through their eyes and through the visual arts. Some are cognitive learners; they attend a lecture or traditional Bible study and process the material through the cerebrum. Others are kinesthetic learners and are most affected by doing, by interaction, by involvement, by immersion in a situation. It is likely that we all learn through a combination of these approaches, with one approach being primary. At any rate, the First Church congregation heard the Matthew texts in a traditional Bible study setting, sitting in a circle around Pastor Dollarhite.

How *do* we "go into the world" of Comanche, Oklahoma? There are fourteen other churches in town. What is our ethical responsibility? Who is the stranger? How can Christ be present in such hard times? Why would God allow such suffering and poverty anyway? How do we make disciples and where do we find Christ? How will our church increase love of God and love of neighbor?

The church began with a free neighborhood breakfast the last Saturday of each month. The pastor quickly learned where the power resided in his congregation—within the leadership of the finance and administrative boards. The chairpersons of both committees had served on those committees for years and held the authority to approve or veto any proposal. On the first Saturday of the neighborhood breakfast, as the pastor had anticipated, the two powerful families could not work together. The matriarch of each of the warring families knew exactly how the breakfast should be prepared. When there were too many in the church kitchen, two separate teams were formed around this culinary conflict. Using a rotation system, both families were given equal control.

The church placed ads in local newspapers and posted signs—*Free Breakfast*. After a few months, fifty to sixty people were attending the free breakfasts. The breakfast committee met for evaluation and ways to improve the free breakfast. Interestingly enough, they decided to take away the word *free*. The committee also decided to invest money in a larger sign that had greater visibility to passersby. The new sign read as follows: "YOU'RE IN-VITED . . . COMMUNITY BREAKFAST SATURDAY 8 A.M.–10 A.M." Attendance increased to eighty persons, then 125. The committee discovered the power of naming. "Persons within a small community, we found out, feel that they want to be able to fend for themselves and not take a handout. Many of the younger families say they would rather do without than ask. Some feel that coming to get a free meal singles them out among the community. It was amazing the amount of difference we noticed after changing the name and the sign."[6]

However, as the outreach expanded, the reflections deepened in the congregation. To whom and for whom are we ministering? Are we doing this just to expand our church? Are we doing this for the money? Is this mission for our own glorification? The cacophony in Comanche, that is, the grating questions and shrill sounds of disagreement, took another turn. Members mumbled that they had worked so hard to make the breakfast work that they were too tired to start another ministry. Pastor Dollarhite then stressed the cost of following the Great Commission.

This complicated and true case has a hospitable outcome. Now, 125 eat breakfast at the church each Saturday, staying for two hours to visit with one another, as in a local coffee shop. The church is finding other ways to feed people, especially schoolchildren who often go hungry on weekends. A Bible study or devotional is an optional time of teaching; in other words, there is no force-feeding of the gospel message. If you had asked two years ago whether there was a Methodist church in town, the response would most likely have been, "We have a Methodist church here?" Now, Pastor Dollarhite hears the reply, "Yeah, that's where the breakfast is held each Saturday."

Contemporary renditions of practical theology combine practice, or *praxis*, with theological reflection.[7] Upon reflection Christ appears present not only to those being served, but especially to those serving. Rephrased, the church members offering

---

6. Ibid.

7. Rodney J. Hunter has elaborated on the use of the word *praxis* in *Dictionary of Pastoral Care and Counseling*, 92. in the following entry, *PRAXIS/ PRACTICE*: "In clinical pastoral usage, 'practice' basically connotes professional role performance (which need not exclude theoretical understanding and existential commitment). 'Praxis,' following liberation theology, connotes the practice of ministry (or a way of life) emphasizing critical social consciousness, questioning its own power interests and those of others."

food are the needy ones, the ones being blessed in the act of praxis, for they are serving Christ at table. Christ comes in disguise as the hungry. This is an educational moment.

Variations on the Theme: Love of God and Neighbor

First Church in Comanche, Oklahoma, went from a theoretical study of biblical passages, Matthew 25 and Matthew 28, into lived experience, or "praxis." After reading about loving God and neighbor in a Bible study in their church, members were motivated to put theory to practice. *Exegesis* is a "leading out" from an authoritative core, commonly sacred Scripture such as the New Testament. This flow of interpretation and application from sacred Scripture has been the traditional movement in most religious circles.

However, "exegesis of experience" has numerous proponents. In the 1960s, practical theology underwent a renewal. For example, England witnessed the revitalization of practical theology as theology gained insights from the social sciences and engaged practice.[8]

Practical theologians began to lead out from encounters with suffering and illness, particularly mental illness. Anton Boisen, one of the founders of the Clinical Pastoral Education movement in the United States and Canada, worked at Worchester State Hospital. He "exegeted" from the lives of his patients who were suffering from mental illness. Theologian Seward Hiltner interpreted psychology and sociology in relation to theology. He understood Christian truth to be informed by God's revelation within the immanence of contemporary experience. Theologian Charles Gerkin, among others, extended the insight of the person as a *living human document*. The newfound reciprocity between the person as living human document and Scripture as holy document resulted in new vistas in practical theology. As exegesis applies to Scripture as document and humankind as living human documents, practical theology becomes "critical engagement with the interface between

---

8. Ballard and Pritchard, *Practical Theology in Action.*

the word of God as revealed through Scripture and the work of God taking place in and through the church in the world."[9]

The exegesis of experience has been fine-tuned by feminists with their research methods, using gender analysis for emancipatory praxis.[10] Theologians who are womanist have added racial analysis to gender analysis as they handle experience, their tradition, and Scripture.[11]

Some practical theologians, called liberation theologians, utilize a Marxist perspective to inform the move from praxis to theory in such a way that the power of naming and proclaiming comes from society's "powerless." Using this methodology, exegesis is done from the academe of the underprivileged. Postcolonial practical theology finds its interpretive center among the formerly "colonized," who become the locus of a new kind of power and perspective.

Whereas the purpose of the church and ministry was summarized as love of God and neighbor, feminists and womanists are leading the way to interpret more thoroughly such biblical passages as Luke 10:27: "You shall love the Lord your God with all your heart, and with all your soul, and with all your strength, and with all your mind; and your neighbor *as yourself*" (emphasis added).

The parable of the good Samaritan illustrated this interplay of love of God, self, and neighbor. The story follows the injunction of three loves. While caring for the wounded, the good Samaritan enlisted the aid of an innkeeper, left the wounded person at the inn, and finished her journey. In this way, the Samaritan balanced care of other with care of self. The Samaritan loved herself by finishing her pilgrimage, by resting herself at the inn before completing her journey, by distributing the responsibility of caring for others in an example of teamwork with both beast of burden and innkeeper, and by following up responsibly with aftercare. She would return

9. Anderson, *The Shape of Practical Theology*.

10. Couture, *Blessed are the Poor?*; Ackerman and Bons-Storm, *Liberating Faith Practices*.

11. Holmes, *Joy Unspeakable*.

and repay.[12] The purpose of the church and its ministry includes a nonnarcissistic love and a respect for self. As theologian and womanist Karen Baker-Fletcher concludes, "Even Jesus seemed to recognize how self-interested we humans are. But there is something positive about that. If we truly know how to love ourselves, the way God loves us and we love God, then we ought to know how to love our neighbors. That knowledge about love is in us and we need to act on it."[13]

Exegesis grows increasingly sensitive to cultural context. Contrast this once again to the historical forces that have shaped theological learning: "Protestant theology was based in biblical exegesis. From the base of biblical studies, Protestant students learned dogmatics and history of doctrine . . . Everything flowed from the scriptural base, which was understood as the normative foundation of scripture."[14] In practical theology in the twenty-first century, there is a revitalizing awareness that the "exegetes" herald from different cultures. More voices take on exegetical authority, more languages become the primary language, and more research disseminates multicultural or intercultural interpretation.[15]

Future questions for the field of practical theology cluster around the multicultural nature, the international audience, and the organic unity of the field. (1) How shall a multicultural or intercultural context influence "exegesis" and practical theology? (2) As variety increases in the different methods of "exegesis" described above, will there be a means of organic unity within the field of practical theology? (3) How will practical theology be related to other disciplines in the academy?

Exegesis in a literal sense means "to lead out" or "to interpret." Often, this evokes an image of leading from one location to another, as from experience to text or from text to experience.

12. Stevenson-Moessner and Glaz, *Women in Travail and Transition,* 200–211.

13. Baker-Fletcher, *Sisters of Dust, Sisters of Spirit.*

14. Berling, "Theological Learning," 49–50

15. Andrews, *Practical Theology for Black Churches;* Pak et al., *Singing the Lord's Song in a New Land;* Lartey, *In Living Colour.*

By contrast, in theatre or dance or symphony, principal players or dancers or musicians can enter the stage from various wings and still participate in the central dance or drama or concert as it unfolds. A challenge for future practical theologians is composing a methodology for "exegetes" who may lead out from different directions yet still participate in God's drama or dance or music on center stage. As practical theologians lead out from east, west, north, and south, with different movements of method, will there be hospitable space for all of the variations? Referring to hospitality as a cardinal virtue in the academy of learning, John B. Bennett presents hospitality as more than generic openness. "[Hospitality] recognizes the particularity of others as part of the broader interdependence of being and the interconnectedness of learning that characterizes the depths of our reality."[16]

In closing, let us turn to *Shoemaker Martin*,[17] based on a story by Leo Tolstoy. In this classic narrative of a Russian cobbler, the reader witnesses the movement from biblical text to experience, then back to biblical text with renewed understanding. The theme of hospitality to others, even the strangers, as biblical knowledge becomes lived knowledge is demonstrated by Martin's attentiveness to "interruptions" in his day.

Shoemaker Martin lived in a basement apartment where he could see the feet of the passersby. Given his occupation as shoemaker, Martin knew most of those feet.

Martin worked hard all day repairing shoes. At night, he lit the lamp, drank tea, and took down his big Bible from a shelf. On this particular night, he read the story of the rich man who invited Jesus into his home. Wondering how he, Martin, would welcome Jesus into his basement apartment, he fell asleep.

During the snowy night, Martin heard a voice: "watch the street tomorrow, because I shall be coming."[18] He went back to sleep. The next morning, Martin awoke with anticipation of a visit from a stranger, a special stranger. He heard footsteps outside, but

---

16. Bennet. *Academic Life.*

17. Tolstoy, *Shoemaker Martin.*

18. Ibid, 5.

recognized only shivering Stefan the street sweeper. Martin invited him in, to sit by the fire and sip tea. Later in the day, while drinking his cabbage soup, Martin noticed a thin woman huddled against the building with an infant in her arms. Her shabby dress was not adequate to protect them both. So Martin invited the two of them inside, gave them hot soup, his old coat, and some money for future needs. Later in the day, Martin heard shouting outside. A hungry boy had stolen an apple from a market woman. Martin helped the two reconcile. That night, in his empty apartment, when the day was done, Martin had the sense that someone was moving behind him. A voice whispered: "Martin, didn't you recognize me?" Stefan the sweeper stepped out of the shadows smiling. "This was me too," said the woman with the baby. "And this was me as well," said the market woman and the poor boy. They were all beaming, then they vanished from the room.

Martin realized his dream had been fulfilled. Jesus had visited him that very day, and Martin had taken Jesus in without knowing. His Bible fell open to the reading for the night: "Inasmuch as you have done it unto the least of these my brethren, you have done it unto me."

In conclusion, I am proposing that the purpose of the church and its ministry, as well as the goal of theological education, is to increase among humankind the love of God, the love of neighbor, and the love of self. This can only be lived with the hospitality of a generous expectancy that we shall encounter Christ in many guises. Love of God is an a priori understanding in the tale of Shoemaker Martin. Love of neighbor is a developed theme in the story. The more elusive of the three loves—love of self—is subtly introduced. It is the experience of God beaming, of God gleaming, of God visiting, of God present. This is not narcissism or selfishness. It is the perception that I am of great value and immense worth to God. It is the conviction that I have absolute value as opposed to relative value because I have been created to receive God's presence.[19]

19. Allen, *Love*, 21.

As in a concert, variations on the theme—love of God, love of neighbor, love of self—are not competitive or contending for attention. Rather, they interplay with and engage each other in what could be termed a divine harmony.

STANZA 3

Movements

INTRODUCTION

It did not start with the affair. No, Katie's affair was a manifestation of her slowly developing malcontent, her hatred of her angry spouse, her depression and despair, her sense that marital life was over. Recounting all her delusions about a good marriage, she concluded, "The impulse to marry would come from the same place as the impulse to drink a bottle of bleach."[1]

In their marital distress, while Katie takes a lover, her husband David finds an indigent spiritual healer named GoodNews. GoodNews cures David's bad back, coaches him in a positive outlook on life, and helps him "be good." "How to be good" entails giving material possessions away, opening up David's home to the homeless and the delinquent, campaigning for the rights of the dispossessed, and changing the neighborhood. David and Good-News call a meeting of the neighbors and convince nine families to take in nine children who have been living on the streets. Although

1. Hornby, *How to Be Good*, 107.

several of the children act out in vandalism and theft in their adoptive homes, four children are "saved" from a street life forever and given many chances in life.

Overwhelmed by her husband's spiritual conversion, Katie attends an Anglican church with a scanty and aging population. It is her first attempt at worship in many years. Katie says of the church service, "It all feels a long way from God. . . It feels sad, exhausted, defeated; this may have been God's house once, you want to tell the handful of people here, but He's clearly moved, shut up shop, gone to a place where there's more of a demand for that sort of thing."[2] Days later, the vicar described as "a middle-aged lady who seems vaguely ashamed of her beliefs," turns up in Katie's medical practice. The vicar did not know Katie was a medical doctor, nor had she even noticed Katie in the vast church on a previous Sunday. The vicar comments, "Basically I no longer believe in what I am doing, and I think it's all a waste of time, and my body knows it. So I feel ill every day."[3]

The novel *How to Be Good* raises questions that are germane to practical theology. Of most interest to me was the central question of the novel: how is one good? The converted life of David and the example of his mentor GoodNews are not too far removed from that of Shoemaker Martin, based on a story by Leo Tolstoy and recounted in the previous chapter. In addition to variations on the theme—love of God, love of neighbor, love of self—which were discussed in the previous chapter, are there perhaps also differing movements in the themes and in the parable of the Good Samaritan itself that vary in tempo or pace? Let us look for distinctive movements in the following case titled "Serve the Somalians."

Prairie Chapel Baptist Church attempts to be "good" through service to others. The parishioners in the Missionary Society genuinely start their project out of love of neighbor. As you remember, the purpose of the church and its ministry was summarized earlier as the increase among people of the love of God and neighbor.[4]

2. Ibid, 233.

3. Ibid, 253.

4. Niebuhr, *The Purpose of the Church and Its Ministry*, 31.

However, in many well-intentioned congregations, the tempo begins to slow almost to a premature ending. If theology is the music of religious inquiry, is it possible that hope or empowerment or joy may quicken the tempo? Equally valid and relevant to the ensuing case study is the question: if theology is the music of religious inquiry, is it possible that disillusionment or powerlessness or suffering may slow the pace to the point of hopelessness or early closure or even death?

ADAGIO, ANDANTE, ALLEGRO, PRESTO, LARGO

Movements or passages in music vary in tempo or pace. From *adagio* to *andante* to *allegro* to *presto*, we hear the pace quicken. With the tempo *largo*, we feel the pace diminish. The same movements can occur in practical theology. In the case study below, you will witness the deceleration of pace and activity into the languid tempo called *largo*. The retardation of movement is tied to context, to ecclesiology, to distribution of power, to orchestration of Project Rescue. The importance of all members of the "orchestra" becomes obvious as the orchestra is eclipsed by an unfortunate solo performance.

Project Rescue, involving the transportation of a refugee family, begins with a slow movement of pastoral initiative, with an *adagio*. The pastor of Prairie Chapel Baptist Church recommends to the Missionary Society that they participate in the Somali Bantus refugee program. It is understandably hard if not impossible for the members of the Missionary Society to imagine such a relocation as the Somalians will experience. It is equally challenging for them to speculate on their role in this cultural upheaval and transplantation of the Somalians. The conversation within the church involved resistance, defense mechanisms, dialogue, and eventual consent to become involved. This stage is *adagio*, a slow tempo towards participation.

The pace quickens slightly when Alice as head of the Missionary Society does her best to involve the congregation in the support of *one family* by donating fifteen hundred to sixteen hundred dollars per month to the family's upkeep. The consolidation of the overwhelming needs of only *one refugee family* helps contain the congregation's anxiety over the cultural and financial hurdles. The specific amount suggested for monthly maintenance of this family helps move the congregation forward on this project. This phase of movement is *andante*, a moderately slow movement in the music of ministry.

More activity occurs when Alice informs the congregation they will be responsible for furnishing and setting up the family's apartment and for providing daily transportation. The pace becomes energized as Alice helps the group envision a limited goal, and there is a brief period of energy with a brisk tempo— *allegro*. An agency called Interfaith Ministries is to help in this undertaking.

A crisis begins to build when only twenty people show up for the orientation meeting. A crisis *crescendo*, or increase in intensity, surges when the faithful few in the congregation are exposed to the cultural differences between them and the Somalians. For example, typically, Somalians cook over an open fire; they do not use ovens, can openers, spatulas, and such. Hence, the congregation has already furnished the apartment kitchen with useless items. At the second orientation, only five people return. This period is filled with *staccato* notes, which are sharp sounds intended for disconnection. The congregation feels confused and frustrated, leading to sharp comments and a sense of alienation from the project.

The climax comes when the Somalian family arrives at the airport—a young mother of three carries one small bag; her baby's diaper has not been changed since the family left New York City. All the way to Oklahoma, the family has not understood one word, nor have they been understood. The only greeters from the church are the pastor, the pastor's spouse, Alice, and a young couple.

For the next four to six months, Alice is often alone in caring for this family. The congregation goes on with their normal activity without ever inquiring about the fate of the Somalians. The congregation had been willing to give money, but they did not perceive the enormous expenditure of prolonged time and presence. How did this movement that began in a chorus of volunteers end in a solo performance? Now, the ministry of mission is at a slow and tedious pace, *largo*.

This case stimulates us to examine our ecclesiology, or our understanding of *church*. It raises issues in leadership (lay and clerical) and church administration. It causes us to consider the church and its ministry. Liberation theology stresses the priority and preference of the poor and disenfranchised and the church's obligation to stand alongside those suffering. When this case became a part of the seminary classroom, the presenter of the case took us through the movement of practice-theory-practice as she experienced it in "Prairie Chapel Baptist Church."[5] This structure of practice-theory-practice and "the movements of theological reflection in all religious activity" is introduced by Don Browning in *A Fundamental Practical Theology*.[6] As Browning describes three religious communities, he argues, "both practical theology and the description of situations proceed as dialogues or conversations."[7] In a similar way, students have offered the experiences of their religious communities in this volume through the methodology of actual cases. As their communities continue the pursuit of practical wisdom (phronesis),[8] may we as readers follow both the case, "Serving the Somalians," and the movements of practical reason: practice-theory-practice.

SERVING THE SOMALIANS

Adagio is a slow warm-up phase that begins with the practice of the decision making involved in launching a new ministry. Ideally, the religious community or representatives of that community will be involved in this phase. Hopefully, the pace will quicken as

---

5. Daniels, "Project Rescue."

6. Browning, *A Fundamental Practical Theology*, 9.

7. Ibid, 15.

8. Ibid, 10. Browning references the sermon on the mount, Matt 7:24.

practice enlivens theory, which emboldens practice. As we reflect on this warm-up phase, let us remember that the project called "Serving the Somalians" began with a solo recommendation from the pastor of Prairie Chapel Baptist Church to Alice, president of the Missionary Society. The recommendation was this: to participate in the Somali Bantus Refugee program.

It is significant to note the context in which this solitary request came. The Missionary Society in this church is a powerful organization—an active ministry on the local, district, and national level of the church. It is composed of women only. Membership is a status symbol because of the monetary power and prestige of the Missionary Society. Normally, the membership elects the president. However, at Prairie Chapel Baptist Church, the pastor took power away from the organization and nominated the president, Alice. The Missionary Society then confirmed the nomination.

When Alice presented the pastor's plan for "Serving the Somalians," the Missionary Society accepted the plan without question. Although the refugee relocation was intended for the entire congregation's participation, the Missionary Society was to "spearhead" the project. Alice was new at this, yet she tried with all her might to elicit the entire Society's membership in the outreach efforts. After the Society meeting, Alice made an announcement to the whole church that they were to be involved in this mission project. There is a slow movement toward church-wide participation; this stage is called *adagio*, a warm-up phase.

Andante is a slightly faster pace although still a moderately slow movement in the music of ministry. To increase the pace, Alice set a financial goal for the congregation: to raise fifteen hundred to sixteen hundred dollars per month to subsidize the Somalians. Understandably, there would be trips to the Social Security Office, to the Health Department, to employment-training classes, to the grocery store and pharmacy. The congregation could imagine these practical necessities. Church members started to envision what their participation would entail and began to display some enthusiasm. A brief period of energy ensued; this brisk tempo is *allegro* in ministry. Alice contacted Jamie at Interfaith Ministries, an agency that would be arranging transportation of the refugee family to the United States. Interfaith Ministries helped refugees who had fled persecution based on race, religion, or political oppression to relocate from refugee camps and transition to the United States. Interfaith Ministries depended on local congregations like Prairie Chapel Baptist Church to be partners in the relocation. The pastor, Alice, and Jamie were all pleased at the animated show of enthusiasm from the church members at Prairie Chapel.

However, the pace or tempo alters yet again. The first orientation meeting draws only twenty people from the congregation, not the large turnout expected. All twenty of the respondents are female. Their questions are as follows: What household items should we purchase for them? Do they use electrical appliances or an oven? What kinds of foods should we buy? What is their religion? Do they speak any English?

Meanwhile, Jamie, the director of Interfaith Ministries, along with another member of her staff, Michel, tried to convey what life had been like for the Somalians: survival with simple skills , their preference for stews, and their inability to speak any English. Jamie saw fear on the faces of the twenty women present. Jamie consoled them with the fact that there would be an interpreter to assist. Also, Jamie reinforced the great need for visitation of this family. In fact, the sole criterion for the Matching Grant Fund supplied by the government for this family was congregational visitation. In short, the connection between congregation and Somalians was their only lifeline. Panic began to form in the audience. An explicit film on life in Somalia only added to the congregation's anxiety.

At the subsequent meeting, only five parishioners came. This meeting revolved around the sign-up sheet for volunteers to help in practical ways: teach the family how to develop hygienic protocol, show them how to use a phone and fill out job applications, explain the maze of American customs, and so on. The parishioners were overwhelmed.[9] The ranks of three hundred "invested"

9. Transplanting from one culture to another is an extremely complicated movement. For further discussion on the complexity of receiving those who are uprooted see chapter 3 of Stevenson-Moessner, *Portable Roots,* 29–41.

members had thinned to an anxious but dedicated five people. The tempo is laced with *staccato* notes, sharp-edged sounds that can seem discordant. This mood shift reflected the confusion and disconnection within individuals in the congregation, and they distanced themselves from the project.

As the tension of congregational cacophony surges, the forward movement of the Somalian family continued. As Alice became primary caretaker for this disoriented family, she was often alone in her efforts. Perhaps out of embarrassment, members of the congregation ignored the Somalians and stopped inquiring about the denouement of this drama. What had started as a complete orchestra ended in a solo performance with Alice. This slow and lethargic pace is *largo*.

PRACTICAL THEOLOGICAL MOVEMENTS

Practical theology concerns itself with movement and direction. Understanding the flow of power adds another dimension, and hence another resource, to reflecting on the practice of ministry. Quite often, those with power to influence affect the flow of the action. Notice that in the case of "Serving the Somalians," the decision to adopt this outreach project comes from the minister and moves to Alice, whom he has handpicked, then to the Missionary Society, then to the congregation. The minister usurped the power of the Missionary Society to elect their own president. This minister continued to act in a way that has been labeled *colonial*, which is reminiscent of a period marked by a monopoly of privilege. The term *colonial* also harkens to a time when this assumed privilege was exploitative. Thus, the minister in this case has acted—whether consciously or unconsciously—as the sole authority and repository of power. This grandiose manner can be exhibited by an individual, a group of individuals, an organization, or a nation. It is the antithesis of practical wisdom emanating from a religious community itself.

Postcolonial practical theology introduces the concept of hospitality and with it the ideal of companionship. John Bennett has deemed hospitality an "essential virtue"[10], claiming that hospitality involves relinquishing defense and protective mechanisms. "To practice hospitality is to share with others in ways that involve receiving. Consequently, practicing hospitality can threaten our stability and control. Truly to share is to invite others into our world, eventually allowing their strangeness and unfamiliarity to affect and engage us."[11]

In the case of "Serving the Somalians," hospitable engagement could only occur if the minister relinquished his control of the Missionary Society and allowed for genuine engagement. This inversion of the traditional or colonial pattern might be challenging, uncomfortable, or enriching—or all of the above. It could result in a mutuality of respect in ministry that is taught in Ephesians 5:21, in a preliminary imperative that introduces the controversial household codes. "Be subject to one another out of reverence to Christ" (v. 21).

An inversion of power has to take place for the world to see how Christ loved the church. The postcolonial mind-set disuses the imagery of slaves and servants and instead prefers the imagery of friends. No clearer is that explained than in John 15:12–15.

> This is my commandment, that you love one another as I [Jesus] have loved you. No one has greater love than this, to lay down one's life for one's friends. You are my friends if you do what I command you. I do not call you servants any longer, because the servant does not know what the master is doing; but I have called you friends, because I have made known to you everything that I have heard from my Father.

In microcosm, the minister of Prairie Chapel Baptist Church ignored the thoughts and feelings of his most active members and instead had them do his bidding. He denied the Missionary Society their designated authority, thus rendering them less powerful. Perhaps if he had relinquished control to Interfaith Ministries, able staff persons like Jamie could have listened to and interacted

10. Bennet, *Academic Life,* 46.

11. Ibid, 48.

with the frightened volunteers. Reframing the project as a time of learning *from* the Somalians could have lessened the anxiety over the enormity of the task. Granted, there must be leadership in such projects, but leadership does not come in the guise of the authoritarian taskmaster or unimaginative composer. Christ calls forth a new way of composing and creates a fresh score.

Religious educator Susanne Johnson notes that the church has often developed a *service-delivery paradigm* in remembering the poor, like the Somalians. According to Johnson, this is not the servanthood model of Christ.[12] The reality of the poor can only be seen from the perspective of the poor.[13] Thus, ministerial outreach needs to be conceived from the perspective of those being served. How could, for example, the Somalians be empowered? Who could translate this perspective to the Missionary Society at Prairie Chapel Baptist Church? Were there already other refugees in the town who could speak for the ones yet to come? The members of Prairie Chapel would then be the *recipients* of care and learning. They would be adventurers in the new region of cross-cultural encounter. The education would be far more extensive than in the average Sunday school class. Refugees like the Somalians would be the educators. This shift in power in itself relieves the anxiety of not knowing.

Dr. Johnson wrote from her locus as a white female from a poor, working class family on the lower rungs of a class-ridden society.[14] She has earned the right to conclude, "Only persons already over-privileged by power can pretend its unimportance."[15] Johnson calls for visional ethics to conceive *outreach* from the vantage point of the needy ones. Of course, in the case of "Serving the Somalians," this vantage point is primarily the Somalian family and the baby with the soiled diaper. However, I suggest similar visional ethics to perceive *inreach* to the location of the unnamed needy, this time, the frightened parishioners and the insulated minister

12. Johnson, "Remembering the Poor," 199.

13. Ibid, 201.

14. Ibid, 204.

15. Ibid.

of Prairie Chapel. As the minister is coached to release his power over, as the members are encouraged to become learners, the *service-delivery paradigm* stands a chance of being transformed.

PRACTICAL THEOLOGICAL REFLECTIONS

Although Jamie and her staff person had tried to explain something about the Somalians, the few members of the Missionary Society willing to assist were dumbfounded by the daunting assignment. "The refugees were people of color. Yet this congregation (of color) viewed them as others. The members who came to the meeting were uncomfortable with their language, lifestyle, and religion. Theologically, they were not prepared to accept these people on common grounds."[16]

According to theologian Peter C. Phan, there is no common ground, only a state called "betwixt and between." The Somalians, in this case, would be in a psychological and cultural space (or nonspace) between their homeland and American mainstream society. According to Phan, research refers now to their "adaptation" to and "incorporation" into American society, "which no longer possesses a single core culture but many mode-diverse cultural matrixes."[17]

This space between two lands or countries is likened to an interstice, or crack, between cultures. Sociologist Ruth Hill Useem describes this as a third culture or hybrid culture.[18] Phan depicts this intercultural space as a matrix with a womb-like, generative possibility. It would be difficult enough for the Somalians to enter this state called "betwixt and between," but it would be almost inconceivable for the average church member at Prairie Chapel Baptist Church to enter this interstitial culture. Church members were being asked to enter a frighteningly foreign situation without guides. It is no wonder that fear overcame them.

16. Daniels, "Project Rescue," 5, 6.
17. Phan, *Christianity with an Asian Face*, 6.
18. Useem, "The American Family in India," 132–45.

How might a theologian best enter the land of "betwixt and between?" First, it would be with humility and with an eagerness to learn. The vision of our call to service would be dialectically related to the discernment of this particular context, that is, the worldview of the transnational migrants or refugees.[19] In a way, the Somalians would serve the congregation and deepen their theological reflection. As theologian Judith Berling concludes,

> What makes theological learning distinctive is its development of Christian character, *habitus*, or wisdom, the deepening of Christian understanding and of Christian lives. As the theological learner learns more about the context of her Christian life—including the impact of religious diversity in it—that learning is folded back into her reappropriation of what it means to be Christian, her sense of the Christian tradition and its language of self-understanding. Thus the theological learner does not merely learn other religions, but re-appropriates her learning into Christian reflection and self-understanding, as "suggestive possibilities" or "spiritual regret" in some other form.[20]

Instead of the top-down movement of power, we have a circular movement in place. In the case of "Serving the Somalians," one theme, that of service to others, emerges as dominant. This could be restated as "how to be good as God is good." However, upon encountering difference (for example, these people cook over an open fire and are not overdependent on gas and electricity) and discerning the particular context of the Somalian family (for example, the young mother is unfamiliar with disposable diapers because she has not lived in a throwaway culture), the theme of servanthood or service takes on variations. Perhaps the Prairie Chapel congregation has something to learn from the Somalians; perhaps service will flow both ways. The blending of this theme will occur when Prairie Chapel members and Somalians can call each other friends and not servants, hopefully in two languages.

19. Wood, *Vision and Discernment*.

20. Berling, *Understanding Other Religious Worlds*, 63.

This surfacing of themes, rising variations on the theme, weaving of themes, and blending of themes is a means of transformation. Although the tempos will fluctuate, the movement goes from practice to theory to (renewed and wise) practice.

In the novel *The Passion of Artemesia*, Susan Vreeland tells a story of costly practice. Outside Rome, at the modest convent of Santa Trinita, Sister Paola recounted how Sister Graziela had died. Sister Graziela snuck out of the convent to see the art of Rome. It was 1631, and the plague was widespread in the city. Yet Sister Graziela's need to see Michelangelo's *Pietà* and Bernini's altar canopy at St. Peter's Cathedral overcame her fear of infection. On her last nocturnal excursion, the aging sister walked the Via Appia and found the spot where Peter saw Christ. Her feet felt warm with God's love. On her return to the convent in the cloak of night, she saw a dying man under the Arch of Constantine. With the love of God compelling her, she whispered the Lord's Prayer in the man's ear, then touched him with the sign of the cross. This touch had a great cost. Three days later, Sister Graziela succumbed to the plague.[21]

Seeking to love God and neighbor beckons us toward boundary crossing, although crossing the boundaries in practical theology does not always lead to such extreme consequences as seen with Sister Graziela. In other words, it does not necessarily create a funeral dirge. However, there is risk in loving God and in loving neighbor in that the self, our self, may be changed. After all, this is the purpose of the church and its ministry. Boundary crossing gives the church more opportunities to be in relationship. This connectedness can yield increase in the love of God and neighbor, sometimes with risk but always with movement. In the end, the purpose of the music of ministry is to hear the overture of God.

---

21. Vreeland, *The Passion of Artemesia*, 288–91.

STANZA 4

Discordant Notes

INTRODUCTION

Practical theology is a spiritual symphony that puts faith in action and action in faith. But what occurs when the stranger in the midst of our ministering is dishonest? A pastor recounts the appearance of a stranger who claimed to have terminal cancer, who needed help getting to his family in Georgia. After the worship service, other pastors and congregations in town gave similar accounts of the appearance of this same stranger, also begging in their midst. How do we minister in this situation?

THE CONNED CONGREGATION

The church often uses the image of the good Samaritan who stopped for a stranger as a picture of caring. In this familiar parable, robbers have left a man near death by the side of the road. Religious officials pass the wounded victim; they are fearful of being contaminated. After all, he has been severely beaten. Perhaps he is dead. Of all people, a Samaritan interrupts his journey and ministers to the desperate stranger. Then, the Samaritan places the wounded on his beast of travel, heads for an inn, and turns the care of the man over to the able innkeeper. The Samaritan rests for the night, offers to return and repay any expenses, and finishes his journey.[1]

Pastors teach their congregations to be like this good Samaritan. While responding to those in need, parishioners are to react in teamwork with other helping professionals like the innkeeper. They are to take care of themselves while helping others. After all, the good Samaritan not only rested in the inn; she finished her journey. What would have happened if the wounded traveler had robbed the good Samaritan? What would have happened if the abandoned stranger had turned upon and beaten up the Samaritan? What if the Samaritan had never made it to the inn? These questions are preparation for the case of "The Conned Congregation." It is a true story and raises questions for practical theology. Among the numerous questions is surely the notion of evil and "its human manifestation as sin."[2] As James Lapsley noted, "It is a bass note, not the melody."[3] Discordant notes may be considered in a variety of categories, but they are not the divine melody.

John Pinkston had prepared his congregation for outreach in ministry. Granted, John was very young. He was twenty-four at the time and in his first appointment as the pastor-in-charge. He did not have a great deal of pastoral care experience. However, the church was most accepting of his leadership even though he described himself as "young enough to be their grandchild in many cases."

The Sunday service began. The announcements were followed by the Apostles' Creed. Pastor John noticed that during the announcements an unfamiliar vehicle had driven by the church. He could see out the front doors of the church from the pulpit. A stranger entered the church and waited until there was a break

1. Stevenson-Moessner, "A New Pastoral Paradigm and Practice."
2. Lapsley, "Responses, Arguments, Musings, and Further Directions," 244.
3. Ibid.

in the service. Pastor John assumed that the stranger was there to worship. Instead, the visitor revealed that he was trying to make his way to Georgia and needed money for the trip. You see, he had terminal cancer. Pastor John relates, "Immediately my heart broke for him. I am unsure of exactly how these next events took place, but I do know that the Holy Spirit was with us and guiding us. I went down to the altar and prayed with the man."[4] The lay leader continued with the service while Pastor John ministered to the sick and needy visitor. Pastor John recounts, "When we were done praying, I stood up, the gentleman stood next to me and, on the verge of tears myself, asked the congregation to take up an offering for him so that he might be on his way and have the means to get to his family." The congregation collected seventy or eighty dollars. Pastor John continues,

> There was a spirit through the rest of the service that is hard to describe. We felt good about ourselves, and it was almost as if we could feel the in-breaking of the kingdom of God right there with us. I even managed to incorporate what had happened into part of my sermon. There were a couple of lingering doubts in the back of my mind, but they were easily quelled. After the service I received a number of compliments on my handling of the situation—that it was done with great compassion . . . If at this point you are beginning to think that the other shoe is just waiting to drop, then you are right.

In the evening, at Bible study, a couple of his church members reported receiving calls from members of other churches in the area about a man who had come to their church looking for help. This man had stopped at several churches. Through compiling the particulars, it soon became obvious that he was not in need, but had taken advantage of the church members. The church began to talk about what it could have done differently. Pastor John offers,

> The general consensus was that we felt we handled the situation in the best way we could, and probably would have done so again based on the same information. We

4. Pinkston, "What Do You Do When a Stranger Comes into Your Midst?," 5.

helped out with what we could, both spiritually and monetarily. Our position was, and still is, that we would rather help out someone who is taking advantage of us than not help out someone who really needs it. This, I hope, will continue to be my position throughout the rest of my ministry. In light of Christian theology this is the answer when Jesus asks where those were that did not clothe him when he was naked.

Pastor John assessed his church's reaction to the "needy stranger" as consistent with their theology. For the congregation to take up an offering to help someone whom they perceived in need was a "logical position" and "a part of our theology as we are in service to others." Pastor John and the congregation also began to discuss ways they could improve their response. They did not have a lot of structures in place to know how to help. They now have a clothes closet, vouchers for groceries and gas, connections with organizations in the community. Pastor John does not want his church to resemble a funding agency with a deluge of forms to be filled and filed. "When this is the final part of our solution, I believe we cease to be the church. We have become a sterile entity that works as a broker from the 'haves' to the 'have nots.' We are not a part of the people who need our help, but we are one stop on a longer journey." Pastor John wants to offer hope as Christ did and does. If we offer no hope, according to Pastor John, we treat the world as a surface to be cleaned.

> We will take out a sponge, mop, rag, or cleaners and we will take care of the surface mess, but are we reaching down to where the real problems lie? We have developed a practical solution to a problem that all churches face, but have we developed a theological one? How do we restore hope to those who have lost it? Even for those who would seek to take advantage of us, can we not offer them hope? Could they be missing hope as well? Could not their attempts of conning us be a cry for hope?[5]

5. Ibid.

Friedrich Schleiermacher divided the various disciplines in the modern university into two categories: pure and positive sciences. A pure science sought knowledge for the sake of knowledge alone. A positive science, such as law, medicine, and theology, combined various areas of inquiry, often skirting across the pure sciences to seek "a unified whole for the sake of some practical purpose. In the case of theology, the practical purpose for which various topics are combined into a field of study is the preparation of church leadership."[6]

The case of "The Conned Congregation" illustrates the workings of a positive science: theology. The action-reflection that occurred after the visit of the dubious stranger is essential to the maturing preparation of church leadership. The unified objective of the local congregation and Pastor John was to offer hope, the hope of Christ, to the stranger. In spite of the duping and dishonesty, hope was still offered in Christ's name. The consensus of Pastor John's congregation, in reflection on their *praxis*, or action, that Sunday morning, was that they had handled the situation in the best way they could. They would choose the same risky action again, rather than run the risk of unresponsiveness to a person in true need.

We began with the image of a tree to illustrate the way Schleiermacher envisioned the connectedness of the areas of theology. Practical theology was the crown, or the branches and fruit, of the tree. Just as there are discordant notes in music, so are there ill winds that rattle the branches of the tree of theology. This case study with the con artist is one such ill wind. However, Pastor John has this last word: "Now we must put into place not only the correct questions to ask but also better answers to those questions. We must start at the root of the problem so that the tree that grows from those roots will flower and be bountiful and no longer just hanging on to life and blowing in whatever breeze may carry it."[7]

6. Schleiermacher, *Christian Caring*, 18.
7. Pinkston, "What Do You Do?," 5.

THE CONFLICTED CONGREGATION

Enter another stranger who responded to an advertising campaign intended to target those looking for a church home. The main message of the ad was the church's "heart, minds, and doors" were wide open to strangers. The stranger entered on Christmas Eve and stayed. The stranger wore a lovely dress with high-heeled shoes. The hospitality to all humanity sounded easy; the discord came when "she" had the dark shadow of a beard line.[8] How does the church minister (or play) to diverse social constituencies? Can everyone be in the audience? What are the biblical, theological, psychological, and philosophical "scores" of practical theology?

Rodney Whitfield presented this case and set the stage. The minister had preached on the text: Matthew 25:31–46. Christ will separate all people as a shepherd separates goats and sheep. The sheep will be blessed because they saw Christ in the hungry, the thirsty, the stranger, the naked, the sick, the prisoner. The Christian education department has picked up on the theme: hospitality to strangers. The mission and evangelism teams spend money on an advertising campaign, now in its third year. The target market is within a ten-mile radius of this medium-size, suburban, upper-middle-class church. Ads are placed in local newspapers. The date is Christmas Eve, a time when people looking for a church home might be more receptive to an invitation. In past Christmas Eve services, there had been over three hundred visitors to the church. As the printed message said, the church's "hearts, minds, and doors" were open to all. This year, ads were placed in less traditional places in hopes of reaching a younger population. It was also an expectation that less traditional people would come.

The Christmas visitor wore a stylish dress with matching purse. For those up close, like the ushers, it was not hard to see the shadow of a recent beard. "Moreover, this man dressed as a woman was close to six feet five inches tall. The ushers and greeters that night welcomed this individual just as they did everyone

8. Whitfield, "A Case of Hospitality," 1.

else."[9] After the service, several of the ushers and greeters talked to the pastor about this Christmas visitor. The pastor assured them they had done well to offer such hospitality. After all, it was an open church—open to all. Besides, the pastor was doubtful if the visitor would return. It was an upper class, Republican, white, and heterosexual congregation—by and large.

Three months later, Joy, the Christmas visitor, returned to worship. She continued to come faithfully each Sunday morning, sitting by herself on the back row. Most people were friendly to her, but few said more than a hello. Then the pastor's phones started ringing. Parents of small children were the most frequent callers. Where would the visitor go to the bathroom? Depending on which bathroom was used, it would scare their children. Perhaps the visitor would even hurt their children. Some parents were dreading the questions their children might ask. "It was about this same time Joy began to reach out to a few individuals who had treated her with respect and true hospitality. She began asking them how she could become more involved in the church. It was at this point the pastor and church leaders began to make decisions for the best interest of the church and Joy."[10]

The pastor and church leaders asked the individuals who had befriended Joy to approach her and convince her that she needed a new place to worship.

> Joy was a precious gift from God but needed to be in a community of faith that could better minister to her needs and situation. These individuals met with Joy on a couple of different Sundays to visit a couple of different congregations in the area which were known for their hospitality and ministry to the gay, lesbian, and transgender community. It happened that Joy said she liked the second church Joy and her new friends attended. I do not know if Joy still attends church there or what has happened, but these new friends do not talk to Joy anymore. Joy has never come back to the church since.

9. Ibid, 1–2.
10. Ibid, 2.

In theory, the message of hospitality as described in Matthew 25 sounded appealing and unexacting. The church's outreach was grounded in Scripture, reinforced homiletically, and taught in education. The hospitality of open hearts and open minds was an element of the congregation's spirituality. The ethics of inclusiveness became a guiding principle in their decision-making. Yet their attempts at application of these teachings, principles, and ethics left a gap between belief and practice.[11] In her chapter titled "Attending to the Gaps between Beliefs and Practices," Amy Plantinga Pauw states that "in all ecclesial forms, struggles persist over gaps between beliefs and practices."[12] She alludes to the dissonance in Jonah's life: "The war between Jonah's beliefs and practices disfigures his actions: he resists any positive connection between his beliefs in God's mercy and compassion and his practice of testimony."[13]

The conflicted congregation struggled over the decision to find Joy another church home. This struggle was met with both sadness and denial. Some reasoned that their actions had come out of love and hope for Joy. The pastor reasoned that she [the pastor] knew her congregation was not ready to make church a safe place for Joy; therefore, her leadership as pastor in allowing members to help Joy find a safe haven was really the wisest decision after all. Others agonized over their internal struggles involving Christian ethics, reality, and reason. What was the right decision?

This congregation started with theory. It was a theory of hospitality and justice based on several biblical passages, most notably Matthew 25. Then, various committees and programs and persons moved in the direction of a practice of the theoretical hospitality. This is where the dissonance occurs. This is where we hear the "discordant notes." Practical theology is a collaborative exercise between theory and practice. David Tracy has described practical theology in these terms: "*practical theology* is the mutually critical correlation of the interpreted theory and praxis of the Christian fact and the interpreted theory and praxis of the contemporary

11. Ibid, 3.

12. Pauw, "Attending to the Gaps," 35.

13. Ibid, 39.

situation."[14] This critical correlation results in the transformation of the person and in some cases, the community.

Rodney Whitfield believes that through the discomfort of the situation surrounding the visitor named Joy, growth will occur in the church. If so, this growth will come as a result of the dissonance perceived between faith and practice. It will come as members see that their practice is not correlated with their theory or theology. It may come when the spiritual sounds of their lives are perceived as out of tune, or discordant, in a symphony that seeks to blend the notes of faith and action. If so, the movement will proceed from theory to practice to theory. Transformation then occurs to the individual, to the community, and to the theory itself.

In rehearsal, there will be clashing, jangling, and rasping sounds. There may be moments of cacophony, disharmony, and atonality. Sometime, we simply fail. However, with practice and praxis in community, we live in the hope of a day of harmony "so when the next Joy comes to visit, we will be able to welcome her unconditionally and without reservations."[15]

14. Tracy, "Foundations of Practical Theology'" 76.
15. Whitfield, "A Case of Hospitality," 7.

STANZA 5

Symphonic Sound

The concert hall is hushed as the conductor mounts the podium. The first movement of the symphony presents a theme, which is later repeated in various ways through successive movements or variations of the theme. When the voice of one instrument predominates, we hear a solo concerto. We are mindful that the other orchestra members are present, but our attention is fixed on the solo.

SOLO CONCERTO

The following case is like a solo concerto. The weak but articulate solo voice comes from the lips of a woman dying of cancer; she is a living human instrument, playing a final song. The melody is similar to a funeral dirge or an elegy. The solo voice is offering a contrast, or contrapositive statement, to the main melody of life itself. This countermovement of the soloist is heard by a hospice worker and seminary student named Kathleen. The melody of the soloist's last days raises questions for pastoral leadership in particular and for practical theology in general.

Kathleen's former career was in the field of public relations prior to becoming a hospice worker. In public relations, she was accomplished at telling other people's stories in publications designed for her corporate clients. Kathleen had the ability, if not the gift, of narrative and storytelling. In the corporate world, Kathleen was not trained to hear "another person into speech" as the theologian Nelle Morton taught.[1] She had also not been trained to hear the silences before the speaking. This intense listening as if with the ear of God has been underscored by theologian Riet Bons-Storm.[2] This is the listening that is deeply theological.[3] It is not a mimicking of what a person says. It is attentiveness to subscripts, to the story not even born. As a hospice worker, however, Kathleen had been trained in this intimate receptivity, so she could learn her greatest lesson. Kathleen titled this lesson "The Cup of Cold Water." The *cup of cold water* is generally used as a metaphor in theological circles. It is a gift from someone who has enough to share with someone who does not. The metaphor comes from Matthew 10:42 (NIV):

> And if anyone gives even a cup of cold water to one of these little ones because he [or she] is my disciple, I tell you the truth, he [or she] will certainly not lose his [or her] reward.

Mark 9:41 refers to a cup of water in Christ's name.

Usually, for practical theologians a "cup of cold water" is given to one who thirsts. This "thirst" can be physical, spiritual, mental, or emotional. In hospice work, patients live under the death sentence of cancer and are in an "estimated" final phase. Hospice care is usually called in around the last six months of a patient's life. Of course, this is always a physician's best guess. Hospice, then, works with physicians to provide a team of workers for the dying. This team generally includes registered nurses, social workers, volunteers, home health aides, and chaplains. What is

1. Morton, *The Journey is Home*, 128.

2. Bons-Storm, *The Incredible Woman*, 32.

3. Justes, *Please Don't Tell*.

noteworthy about this particular case is that the cup of cold water, in the end, was given not *to* the patient but *by* the patient, Patricia, age sixty, dying from liver cancer. This unexpected movement or countermovement is in accord with the currents in contemporary practical theology. There is a shift away from traditional sources of power and authority; for example, in what is being termed *colonial times* (in other words, when indigenous people were colonized by superpowers and ruling countries), the dominant belief was that the industrial nations gave *cold water* to the underindustrialized. Again, *cold water* is a metaphor and could represent giving food, farm implements, spiritual solace, clothing, or funds. The details may vary, but the flow is always consistent: from the powerful or advantaged to the underprivileged or disadvantaged. Unfortunately, in some cases, with the flow of help or aid comes a sense of power. Equally unfortunate are the stories of the abuse of that power. Therefore, some contemporary practical theologians use the adjective *non-hierarchical* or *non-authoritarian* in their theories and praxis to signal their attempt to distribute the power flow. The goal is to empower the dispossessed, the disadvantaged, the poor, and the underside of elitism. Practical theologians mean to redefine *power* as God-given, innate authority. Those who are illiterate, impoverished, and forgotten have intrinsic validity, power, and worth. Those on the margins of society are offering up lots of "cold water" if those of us who are nonmarginalized would receive. Contemporary practical theologians are open to the image that the cold water flow is abundant from the edges of society because Christ who offers "living water" is drawing from the well (John 4:11). In this Johannine passage, Christ is honoring a marginalized woman of Samaria and requesting water from her.

This is a story from the end of life. Patricia was newly admitted to hospice care. She had been a career woman with a happy marriage and two adored adult children. Patricia desired life, but the brutality of liver cancer relegated her to the last stages of illness. Out of her determination and love of the living, Patricia fought for time. She lived for almost a year. Given her diagnosis, her life expectancy, initially, had been only a few weeks, at best a few months. At least, this was the verdict of her physician. Patricia tried countless types of homeopathic remedies, including experimental prescriptions. She wanted to live.

Kathleen, the hospice worker, became very close to Patricia in this eleven-month battle for life. Kathleen did what she was trained to do; she tried to keep the focus of conversations on Patricia. Yet, each visit, Patricia would take the lead and ask Kathleen questions. Patricia claimed her innate power to compose the score, to write the melody of the moments.

Patricia began to show evidence of physical decline. Kathleen's supervisor gave her a mandate, not a request. Kathleen was required to visit Patricia each day. Patricia's husband, desperate with fear and anticipatory grief was pressuring the hospice staff to do more to help. It is such a cruel intimacy to watch your loved one die. Kathleen could not do enough to meet the family's demands. Kathleen was irritated. It was unheard of for one hospice worker to be required to visit the same terminal patient six to seven times a week. If this did happen, it was expected of the nurses.

Patricia and her husband lived on well-manicured acreage outside Kansas City. The house was a fifty-mile drive each way for Kathleen. Kathleen writes, "Simply put, but not proudly from my perspective, the daily visitation schedule angered me. I recall thinking that my time with Patricia was taking me away from the other 'real' work that needed to be done." Hospice had other patients, yet Kathleen was spending half a day with one!

In addition to Kathleen's ministrations, Patricia's husband was quite attentive to her needs; a support group from Patricia's Episcopal church, as well as friends and numerous other hospice volunteers, visited her. In fact, the church support group as well as the minister also drove fifty miles each time they visited. The visits were staggered so that Patricia would not overly tire from the number of visitors.

One afternoon, when Patricia could hardly talk, she murmured that she had found out something about Kathleen. She had found out from one of the other hospice nurses that Kathleen was thinking about becoming an ordained minister. Patricia asked

Kathleen if that was true. Kathleen tried to avoid the topic in an attempt to prevent nonprofessional self-disclosure or self-revelation. In pastoral listening, the attention is to be focused on the patient or parishioner, not on the counselor or pastor. Kathleen did not think this was the time to talk about her plans. Yet, Patricia persisted in her questioning and announced, "You must do this. You are my minister." Kathleen felt ordained at that moment, and she never forgot that blessing. She recalled that moment as she completed seminary. The day of Patricia's blessing was the day of her anointing. (Kathleen is now a chaplain on an oncology unit.)

She and Patricia said prayers together. Kathleen grew more comfortable with the short then gradually longer periods of silence between them. Then the "heartbreaking climax" came early one morning. Kathleen: "Patricia was actively dying and that's where my story becomes a case in point for theological reflection." Kathleen used the instruction that Patricia was giving her for her own formation and religious rumination. Kathleen recalled that Patricia was a Roman Catholic before she became an Episcopalian. On the last day they sat together, Kathleen asked if she might request Patricia's priest to come and say a blessing, to anoint with oil and pray. Kathleen had Patricia's Roman Catholic tradition in mind when she asked.

Kathleen recorded, "Patricia's response to my presumed 'pastoral' question astonished me. She said, with a tone of clarity and resolve that I can still hear: 'Oh, I suppose you could ask (the church and minister) to come do that for me. But they have been doing those things for me for a long time now. I really haven't gotten too much from the rituals they do for me . . . but I think it has helped them a lot . . . so I've let them do that for me.' " Kathleen was stunned. "Though Patricia had received care from her family, church, and the hospice team, she had allowed us to feel we were ministering to her for our sake. This was not clear to me but a true shock." Who was actually offering the cup of cold water?

> In that moment and for the years that have passed since that day, I have reflected deeply about this experience. Patricia had her pastoral care needs. But in the end, I

think Patricia was the one whom God used the most to help each of us who loved her. I don't think she was a martyr or even meant to be that for anyone. I ask myself now, in light of this personal ministry experience, "What is practical theology?" In this situation, I think Patricia's attention to me and others was the point we all overlooked. The hospice team and her church were doing their best, as was I, to be [expedient] and to meet her emotional, physical, and spiritual needs.

I think each person's intention during that difficult period was meant as a genuine expression of love toward her. I also recognize that we were focused far too much on the "doing" for her. Critical reflection now tells me that Patricia, on a deeper level, had not been heard. I think we were just too busy and too anxious to listen for what she probably desired most and that was—our stillness, our quiet silences. I understand practical theology to be (at a minimum) Christ's love made visible to others. In her story, the doing . . . the trying to give her rituals that she didn't really desire may have caused her more spiritual harm than good.

What questions does this raise for pastoral leadership and pastoral care?

Kathleen regretted not listening more and waiting more for "the open spaces of God's grace. The 'doing' of getting her food she couldn't eat, bringing her music on tape she wasn't able to [hear] . . . may have blocked the deeper needs in her life. She didn't look forward to death, but she faced it with much courage. She wanted to be treated as a member of the living who could still hear and sense what was more important in life. Patricia loved life, and she kept trying to teach us that very lesson." Kathleen concludes that Patricia was both the teacher and the stranger in their midst. She visited Patricia numerous times and thought she knew her. In retrospect, Kathleen concludes, "I had rarely 'seen' her." Kathleen knew of Patricia's strong faith. "I believe Patricia had internalized the Christian rituals of blessings and anointing with oil for healing long ago. As a result, the outward expressions of these rituals had served to help her caregivers at a depth that most of us simply didn't grasp at the time."

Kathleen cites the teaching of Mother Teresa of Calcutta, Missionaries of Charity. "Until you can hear Jesus in the silence of your own heart, you will not be able to hear Him saying, 'I thirst' (in the heart of the poor)."[4] Practical theology can move from action to reflection, from reflection to action, and then repeat itself. The movement is cyclical and circular, not linear. In Kathleen's analysis of her visits to Patricia, she felt she had rushed in to minister before reflecting adequately on what Patricia was needing. In addition, Kathleen highlighted the fact that every person or patient "has a voice . . . a voice that can only be heard for its profundity if one practices a type of listening that reflects God's love. The doing of such reflection is the first, not the second, step in living out Christ's words from the cross, 'I thirst.'" A ministry of presence is attentive to the silence of a parched soul, the arid places of the spirit, the withered will, the shriveled self-esteem. Surely, if actual liquid is needed, the minister or hospice worker responds with the actions appropriate for hydration. However, it is in a ministry of being with someone (ministry of presence) that God leads into a depth of discernment to hear the silences of the soul. This is not dissimilar from a musical score where the silences, the pauses, have their meaning, too

Practical theology has more than one soloist, more than one principal. Even with a solo concerto, other orchestra members are needed. There is often an ascendancy of one section. The percussion will come forward or the wind instruments will take the lead. A lone French horn will arch its melody over the concert hall. A drumroll or the notes of a harp will capture the attention of the audience. All of this is symphonic sound.

Of course, the acoustics need to be of good quality. Only then can the space convey sounds with audibility and accuracy. The role of practical theology is to create and maintain such a space.

4. Petrie and Petrie, "Mother Teresa."

THE CONDUCTOR

Pastoral leadership and pastoral administration may resemble, at times, the role of a conductor. We cannot avoid the theological, even christological, import of the position of conductor. God or Christ may be seen as a unique realization of this creative coordinator, the conductor.[5]

In *Desert Hearts and Healing Fountains: Gaining Pastoral Vocational Clarity*, Victor Hunter takes lessons from the New York Orpheus Orchestra.[6] The mutuality within this musical community and the nonhierarchical role of the conductor is a model for practical theological leadership.

> The point of the conductor of an orchestra is to lead, not to run all over the orchestra pit playing all the instruments. The conductor is to "orchestrate," read and understand the music, know its history and its meanings, give attention to nuances and subtleties, and enable the playing by the orchestra of a great symphony. But for that to happen there must be a host of trained musicians who have a passion for the music, who read and understand it, who also pay attention to nuances and subtleties, and who give voice to their instruments.[7]

Hunter goes on to paraphrase seven principles of such orchestration.

1. Remember that people, or music-lovers, want to hear an orchestra, not an institution.

2. Look for common solutions even in chaos, for chaos precedes the creative act.

---

5. For a similar analogy, that of Christ as "unique realization" of the Samaritan in Luke 10:27, see discussion in Stevenson-Moessner, "A New Pastoral Paradigm and Practice,"103.

6. Hunter, *Desert Hearts and Healing Fountains,* 128. Hunter's illustrations and his seven principles are drawn from a report heard on National Public Radio.

7. Ibid, 128.

3. Accept repetition as a normal occurrence in the music of ministry.

4. Lead by allowing others to take initiative.

5. Develop leaders (musicians) who are flexible, creative, and also collegial.

6. Encourage a free exchange of ideas, or scores.

7. "Understand that God is not necessarily efficient but passionate."[8]

Flexibility in pastoral leadership or conducting allows space for two-part harmony, even three-part harmony. There may be scores of music that require antiphonal responses or alternative tunes. For the practical theologian, this may sound like cacophony at times. However, cacophony precedes harmony and creation.

MUSIC: THE UNIVERSAL LANGUAGE

The orchestra members may sit in the orchestra pit and provide a background for a chorus of singers, an opera, or a dance or ballet troupe. The one commonality among the players and principals is the music itself, which connects all these forms of art and creativity.

Music is a universal language, like prayer. In various cultures, music manifests itself in different forms. In Korean American life, for example, singing is a well-recognized and collective phenomenon. Everyone has at least one song to sing at a gathering; this song is called *ship-pal-bun* (literally meaning "the number eighteen"); it is a favorite song.[9] Korean Americans consider music powerful in their lives. "Most that study Korean culture and religions agree that shamanism is at the core of Korean popular religiosity and popular culture and that Korean arts, including music and dance, developed in the crucible of shamanistic practices."[10] Music becomes a mediation between this world and the next. "Likewise,

8. Ibid. All principles are paraphrased with the exception of the seventh.

9. Pak, et al., *Singing the Lord's Song in a New Land*, 26.

10. Ibid, 260.

Korean American Christians consider music a powerful spiritual resource and appropriate it to meet their needs in faithful living."[11]

Theology is the music of religious inquiry. It is available to all. God has made us to be living instruments, capable of creativity. We are born to investigate our relationship with that Creator God. This investigation is theology; it is especially practical theology.

In 1610, in Brittany, a one-time actress and ropedancer named Juliette, sought refuge in her pregnancy among the holy sisters of the abbey of Sainte Marie-de-la-mer. This story unfolds in Joanne Harris's novel, *Holy Fools*.[12] Juliette recalled an earlier time of imprisonment and her desolation in a cell below a courtroom. She reflected,

> We were guilty. No one would dispute it. . . Someone else—a person of faith—might have found comfort in prayer, but I did not know how to pray. There is no God for the likes of us, Le Borge used to say, for we were not made in [God's] image. We are the holy fools, the half-made ones, the ones who came out broken from the kiln. How could we pray? And even if we could what would we say to [God]?
>
> And so I set my back against the stone and my feet on the baked earth floor, and I stayed there as dawn approached, cradling the new life in my belly and listening to the sounds of sobbing from the other side of the wall.[13]

Our last chapter will address the reality of those like Juliette who consider themselves "half-made fools" unable to pray or sing. How can music be the universal language when all we hear is the "sobbing from the other side of the wall"?

11. Ibid.

12. Harris, "Holy Fools," 76.

13. Ibid.

STANZA 6

Encore

MUSIC: THE UNIVERSAL LANGUAGE

When his son walked onto the stage to play "Estudio" and "Estudio Sin Luz," the notes of these two pieces were most familiar to David. David had always resisted Paul's preference for music over medicine. David had even discouraged Paul's interest in applying to the Juilliard School of Music. David had heard his teenager practice these pieces a hundred times during their recent vacation. Yet this moment, watching his son perform in the auditorium, was different. "Slowly, slowly, David let himself relax into this darkness, closing his eyes, letting the music, Paul's music, move through him in waves. Tears rose in his eyes and his throat ached. He thought of his sister, standing on the porch and singing in her clear, sweet voice; music was a silvery language it seemed she'd been born speaking, just as Paul had."[1] She was a child with Down syndrome, yet she and her nephew, Paul, spoke the same "silvery language." As the Frenchwoman Madame Angellier re-

---

1. Edwards, *The Memory Keeper's Daughter*, 195.

marks in the novel *Suite Francaise* while listening to the German "enemy" soldier playing the piano, "music alone can abolish differences of language or culture between two people and evoke something indestructible within them."[2]

Music is a universal language. I remember sitting in a high balcony seat during the Salzburg Music Festival in the summer of 1970. My friends and I had decided at the last minute to purchase tickets for the Mozart Festival. All that was left were tickets to a Classical Chamber Orchestra playing, of course, Wolfgang Amadeus Mozart. There were three of us: Ceci, Sarah, and me. Ceci had been diagnosed with advanced leukemia. At the time, she was in a state of remission and came to Europe before the disease progressed further. Sarah was a missionary serving in an underdeveloped nation. She joined us in Salzburg to spend quality time with Ceci. The music held the three of us, longtime friends, in an embrace. But it is Sarah who comes to my mind when I recall that night. Having purchased the tickets, I was somewhat embarrassed by the seating arrangement; our bargain tickets put Sarah right behind a huge stone pillar. She could not see the musicians. What I remember with great clarity now, over forty years later, are the tears pouring down Sarah's cheeks as the beauty of the music offered salve to her life of hardship in service. Music offers a healing vocabulary.

Music also offers a familiar vocabulary. On September 11, 2001, I was with my "Pastoral Care and Counseling of Women" class at the Maria Shelter in Dubuque, Iowa. We had planned this site visit to a transition house for women and children moving out of violent conditions, unemployment, or addictions. As our guide took us through the lounge area, the news on television caught our attention. Of course, we saw those early shots of people jumping out of buildings in New York City and the towers crumbling. My class and I were not even certain what we were watching. Later that day, I asked a Methodist minister what she had done for her congregation amid such chaos. In the midst of uncertainty and fear, she opened up church doors and people poured in. Then they

2. Nemirovsky, *Suite Francaise,* 334.

all sat together and sang familiar hymns of the faith. The score, the stanzas, and the substance offered a security to the soul.

Theology is the music of religious inquiry. Practical theology is the music of religious inquiry in cyclical engagement with theory and practice, with practice and theory, with both the orchestra and the audience. The audience participates just as passionately as did David and Sarah, mentioned above. This engagement between orchestra, opera, ballet, or choir and the audience is in no way passive because mutuality depends on active reflection and interior involvement of all parties. All persons are "living human instruments" fashioned by a Creator Conductor to play the music of religious inquiry.

LIVING HUMAN INSTRUMENTS

In practical theology, this ever-deepening reflection is either preceded or followed by action and practice.[3] In some academic circles, the language is that of "action-reflection" or "theory-*praxis*." When practice is involved in political engagement and injustice or social activism, it is often called *praxis*.[4] Sometimes this engagement or formation[5] is life threatening or sacrificial. In the following cases of Elizabeth Cady Stanton, Dietrich Bonhoeffer, the women of Uhuru Park, and Jeannette Noel, I will put a spotlight on these individuals to illuminate or highlight their personal price of *praxis*.

3. Ogletree, "Dimensions of a Practical Theology," 84.

4. Hunter, "Praxis/Practice (Terminology)," 937.

5. Understanding theology as "the work of the people of God" and seeking to relate the academic discipline of theology to worshiping communities of faith, practical theology serves as a vital bridge between the two. In their editorial preface to *Formation and Reflection: The Promise of Practical Theology* (Philadelphia: Fortress Press, 1987), Lewis S. Mudge and James N. Poling offered this definition: "By 'practical theology' we mean that movement among seminary and university and divinity-school faculty which makes the process of *formation* of Christian community and personhood in the world thematic for critical *reflection*" (xiv).

I have chosen four distinct exemplars to broaden accessibility to the field of practical theology and to the price of *praxis*. The first to take a curtain call, or to step into the limelight, is an activist, a feminist, an author, and a reformer: Elizabeth Cady Stanton (1815–1902). Her participation in the reform movement of abolitionism, the annulment of slavery, eventually led to her sharpened theological reflection as evident in a commentary on the Bible. The second person to take a curtain call is a well-known academic, theologian, and author: Dietrich Bonhoeffer (1906–1945). His theological reflection burgeoned in academic circles, including the University of Berlin. From centers of intellectual activity like Tübingen and Berlin and from his exegetical study of Matthew 5 (the Sermon on the Mount), there was a mounting investment in political resistance to Adolf Hitler and the Third Reich to the point of martyrdom. The third and fourth exemplars are less well known . The third is not an individual, but a group of women who organized to challenge dictatorship in Kenya. Their willingness to stand firm in protest, even when attacked by police, served as a catalyst for democratic reform in the country. The fourth exemplar was a contemplative, a rebel, and a Catholic Worker: Jeannette Noel (1916–2006). In her life we see the interweaving of praxis and reflection, as well as her involvement with the *Catholic Worker* newspaper and hospitality ministry. I chose Jeannette and the Kenyan Women because the price of their *praxis* is not widely acknowledged, as compared to those of Bonhoeffer and Stanton.

Elizabeth Cady Stanton

The last three decades of the nineteenth century in the United States were a period of much religious unrest. Americans called organized religion into question, felt the influence of Eastern religions, and challenged biblical infallibility. "American Protestants were compelled to come to terms with new intellectual movements, such as Darwinism, and with new scholarly disciplines, such as anthropology, comparative religion, and biblical criticism."[6]

Into this challenging mix, Elizabeth Cady Stanton assembled nineteen women from the United States, along with a group of international women (Finland, England, Austria, Scotland, and France), to create a "Revising Committee" and to offer an early feminist critique of biblical religion. Their methodology was to underscore all sections of the Hebrew Bible and New Testament that mentioned women or attitudes about women. Then members of the Revising Committee cut out the sections, pasted them on sheets of paper, and commented on all biblical passages. The reflections were from the marginal position of women, although these were educated women. They were marginal to the guilds of professional biblical scholars. The first woman was admitted as member of the Society of Biblical Literature, the guild of biblical scholarship, in 1894. Thus, in the period 1895–1898, when women were excluded from the guild, Stanton and the Revising Committee wrote a woman's commentary to the Bible. Having worked hard in the abolition movement for the freedom and equal rights of slaves, then pouring activist energy into the efforts for women to have the right to vote, Stanton and her committee wrote pointedly to undermine inappropriate use of Scripture that rendered women inferior creatures. For example, commenting on the "nameless women" in Exodus 2, the Revising Committee illustrated the continuation of the invisibility of women in their day: "If we go through this chapter carefully, we will find mention of about a dozen women, but with the exception of one given to Moses, all are nameless. Then as now names for women and slaves are of no importance; they have no individual life, and why should their personality require a life-long name? To-day the woman is Mrs. Richard Roe, tomorrow Mrs. John Doe, again Mrs. James Smith according as she changes masters."[7] Samples of the commentary include the following:

6. Smylie, "The Woman's Bible and the Spiritual Crisis," 307.

7. Cady Stanton, et al., *The Woman's Bible, Part I,* 73.

Our civil and criminal codes reflect at many points the spirit of the Mosaic. In the criminal code we find no feminine pronouns, as "He," "His," "Him," we are arrested, tried, and hung, but singularly enough, we are denied the highest privileges of citizens, because the pronouns "She," "Hers" and "Her," are not found in the constitutions. It is a pertinent question, if women can pay the penalties of their crimes as "He," why may they not enjoy the privileges of citizens as "He"?[8]

Stanton wanted women to become all that the Creator intended them to be. She sought to free women from traditional interpretations of Scripture that encouraged women to be submissive, childlike, docile, and passive. This she saw as "hermeneutical enslavement," in other words, a way of interpreting women as inferior to men, as unequal.

Stanton was especially active in the abolition movement, applying the Decalogue, or Ten Commandments, in Exodus to the institution of slavery. For example, taking the commandment "Honor thy father and thy mother," she wrote: "How can the beautiful daughter of a southern master, honor the father who with cold indifference could expose her on the auction block to the coarse gaze of licentious bidders . . . Or, do you tell us, Sinai's thunders were never meant for [Africa's] ears?"[9] She worked tirelessly against the abuse of slavery; she connected the injustice of the subordination of slaves with the subordination of women. Thus, abolitionism and feminism were both crusades in her praxis.

For her praxis, she paid a price. "The resistance to *The Woman's Bible* was intense, not only from clergymen, but from many women as well. Stanton's attack on the Christian church and on literalism put her out of the mainstream of the women's rights movement; she remained, however, a vital voice. *The Women's Bible* was even denounced by the National American Woman Suffrage Association, of which Stanton was honorary president."[10] Stanton's

8. Ibid, 74.

9. Cady Stanton, "The Slaves Appeal," 5.

10. Stevenson-Moessner, "Elizabeth Cady Stanton, Reformer to

life experience impacted her theological reflection, which then continued to inform her stands for equality and justice. Although her biblical methodology is controversial, it can be said that she heard cries of the excluded, which play to our ears as a lament. In her words, "Our religion, laws, customs, are all founded on the belief that woman was made for man. Come what will, my whole soul rejoices in the truth that I have uttered. One word of thanks from a suffering woman outweighs with me the howls of all Christendom."[11]

Dietrich Bonhoeffer

In 1923, an obscure house painter named Adolf Hitler rocketed onto the scene in Germany with his National Socialist German Workers' Party. Hitler became a national hero. In 1923, the seventeen-year-old Dietrich Bonhoeffer decided to pursue theology, shocking his parents and upsetting his two elder brothers. Bonhoeffer entered the University of Tübingen at a time when Germany was in crisis.

In January of 1933, Adolf Hitler became Chancellor of Germany, and the Third Reich was officially established. The country and the church was riddled with anti-Semitism and other forms of racism. Hilter told his colleague, Hermann Rauschning, before becoming dictator, "One is either a Christian or a German, one can't be both."[12] Hitler intended to stamp out Christianity in Germany.[13] He also isolated and exterminated those whom the state deemed as non-Aryan or as unhealthy Germans. Thus, Jews, gypsies, specially-abled persons, as well as nonconformists of many kinds were put in concentration camps to face extinction.

Dietrich Bonhoeffer's doctoral dissertation, completed in 1927 for the University of Tübingen, was the "Communion of

Revolutionary," 686.

11. Stanton and Stanton, *Elizabeth Cady Stanton*, 2:82.

12. Craig, *Six Modern Martyrs*, 25.

13. Ibid.

Saints" (*Sanctorum Communio*) about the union of Christians through Jesus Christ. Bonhoeffer maintained that this union demanded personal commitment more than a membership card. To obtain a teaching position in European universities, an academic like Bonhoeffer had to write a "second dissertation," or research treatise, called a *Habilitationsschrift*. In this second dissertation, titled "Act and Being" (*Akt und Sein*), Bonhoeffer described the church as a community where each person encounters Christ in the other. After his involvement with the Barmen Confession, a document of the German resistance movement and a founding document for the Confessing Church, which opposed Hitler's ascendancy, Dietrich Bonhoeffer lost his teaching status at the University of Berlin. Bonhoeffer continued to mentor students at Finkenwalde, a seminary for the Confessing Church. At this juncture in his life, Bonhoeffer completed his work on the Sermon on the Mount (Matthew 5); it was *The Cost of Discipleship*, first published in 1937. In this watershed work, Bonhoeffer distinguished between cheap and costly grace. According to Bonhoeffer, Martin Luther's doctrine of justification by faith alone encouraged "cheap grace" in such a way that believers in Christ were relieved of the obligations of discipleship. Costly grace is so named because it costs a person her or his life; it is grace because it ultimately gives that woman or that man the only true life. "Above all, it is *costly* because it cost God the life of [God's] Son."[14] In 1937, Finkenwalde closed by order of the Gestapo.

In 1938, Bonhoeffer established contacts with political opponents of Hitler and involved himself in a plan to kill Hitler. In 1943, the authorities incarcerated Bonhoeffer in Berlin's Tegel Prison. In 1944, he was moved to Gestapo Prison in Berlin, then in 1945 to Buchenwald concentration camp, later to Regensburg, and then to Schoenberg. Bonhoeffer's acts of resistance connected with theological reflection as evidenced in both poetry and song from within the prison walls:"In prison, Bonhoeffer wrote poetry; in prison he sang of a Christianity liberated from the military boot of a contemporary anti-Christ, and of a spirituality sprung from

14. Bonhoeffer, *The Cost of Discipleship*, 48.

ponderous theology and prideful ecclesiastical dogma."[15] Bonhoeffer's poetry moved from praxis to reflection, reflection to praxis, and back again. In one of his best known poems, "Who Am I?," sent to Eberhard Bethge, Bonhoeffer described his confinement "like a bird in a cage, / struggling for breath, as though hands were compressing my throat."[16]

On April 9, 1945, Bonhoeffer left the "cage" of his prison room, felt fingers of threaded rope around his throat, struggled for his last breath, and was hanged at Flossenburg Camp. After the war, when a monument to Bonhoeffer was inscribed on the grounds of the concentration camp, the carved title of "who he was" answers the question of his poem. The inscription could have read "Herr Professor," for Bonhoeffer taught at the University of Berlin. It could have read "Autor," for he wrote many books such as *The Cost of Discipleship* and *Life Together*. Instead, the monument bears these words:

Pfarrer Dietrich Bonhoeffer

That is, *Pastor* Dietrich Bonhoeffer, free in the full embrace of God.

The Women of Uhuru Park, Kenya

A student from Kenya recalled a situation in his country in 1992. The country was under a forced dictatorship. The population increased as did poverty and unemployment. The World Bank and the International Monetary Fund (IMF) placed sanctions on Kenya. Many Kenyans wanted change and a voice in the government; those who spoke out against President Moi often became political detainees.

Wangary Mathai "led a group of women to the Uhuru Park on a hunger strike. They refused to eat or drink demanding the release of all political detainees held without trial. For forty days and nights they camped at the park until on executive order, they

15. Coles, "Preface," 9.
16. Bonhoeffer, "Who Am I?" 189.

were attacked by the anti-riot police in full combat gear. The attack was recorded and broadcast all over the world as police on horses shot tear gas and beat the hungry women who offered no resistance" (student would like to remain anonymous). In response, the women undressed and stood naked before their oppressors. This undressing was the last act left for the women. It was a signal that no more harm could be done. Undressing declares a readiness to die. "The action challenged the aggressor to finish the task . . . It implies as naked one came to earth so also is he/she ready to leave." This act conveys a curse to the aggressor. President Moi received a clear message. "Women old enough to be his mother had shamelessly and publicly declared their willingness to die for the sake of the nation." He convened the Kenya Africa National Union's National Delegate's Conference and recommended a change to the constitution. This decision, as a result of the political activism of the women, would allow Kenya to become a multi-party system.

Jeannette Noel

On behalf of less-recognized persons who pay or have paid a price for the practice or praxis of their faith, I am closing this prelude with a name that is not as well-known as my earlier examples. May this last choice represent countless others who have known the cost of commitment. Jeannette Noel was a worker in the 1970s in the House of Ammon, a fifteen-room farmhouse in Hubbardston, Massachusetts. As a Catholic Worker hospitality house, the House of Ammon was a healing community offering both physical necessities and spiritual hope to those hurting and alone. The Catholic Worker movement, emboldened by the initial work of Dorothy Day and Peter Maurin, has a long history of liberality and hospitableness to those in need. The Catholic Worker movement opened its first house of hospitality in 1933. Today there are over 130 Catholic Worker communities. The House of Ammon, where Jeannette Noel ministered, was just such a restorative community, although there were times of great hardship. Once, even Jeannette's personal furniture was burned and used as firewood by some of the guests at this house of hospitality. Jeannette wrote honestly about her years of service to the homeless, to youth, to those dealing with addictions:

> In seven years it was a home to joy and sadness, and sometimes madness. Always I felt that God was with us. In that time I saw good destroy evil often. I experienced so much in a short time . . . more than most do in a lifetime. We were blessed that these people who felt rejected by society were able, in time, to trust us, even love us. We did not have much of the world's goods to give them, somehow we gave them a place to sleep, food and love. We hope the seed of love planted in them will grow and give them hope wherever they are, and will help them grow and find themselves.[17]

In 1978, a fire destroyed the House of Ammon. Jeannette lost everything. She moved to New York City at age sixty-two and began working for the newspaper *The Catholic Worker*. She handled the mailing addresses and thank you notes, always in a spirit of prayer. She lived in a small apartment at Maryhouse in New York City; her apartment was next to the dining room. She kept her door open and offered her own brand of hospitality, especially to other workers. She practiced centering prayer at 3:00 each afternoon; she gave instructions in meditation. She attended the Church of the Nativity on Second Avenue and took Communion once a week to the elderly and infirm. She took Communion to approximately fourteen people a week even as her body and memory began to decline.[18]

Her last years were spent in Cabrini nursing home. Even there, her coworker Bernard Connaughton described her as a comforting presence to lonely souls. He visited her the night before she died: "She had been on oxygen for several days and was uncomfortable and anxious. She was quiet, but then she suddenly began to sing "Amazing Grace." It was not unusual for Jeannette to sing, but it

17. Connaughton, "Jeannette Noel, 1916–2006," 1, 4.

18. Ibid., 4. These facts are documented by Bernard Connaughton, fellow worker, in his testimonial to her.

came as a surprise as she lay in distress. We sang together. She died the next day and Jane, Amanda, and I sang "Amazing Grace" for Jeannette as she lay in death, in great peace and dignity."[19]

Jeannette's image of God shifted from that of a punitive, angry God to One who loves unconditionally. As she prayed the Psalms, she felt linked to her ancestors in the faith. She knew that God's light penetrated unspeakable evil to call all God's children home to love. She discerned God's presence and support in her life. She remarked, "How could I not love [God]. Now I long for the day [God] will call me home and embrace me with a hug. Only then will I know perfect love and peace. To be reconciled and be with the many I have learned to love in this life. Alleluia."[20]

These lives illustrate the interconnection of reflection-action-*praxis*. There is not one pattern for this interaction. Yet this interaction activates the creative energy of God within God's living human instruments.

Practical theology revitalizes the church as practice and reflection circle back on each other. We must continue to ask: What are the biblical foundations, the historical roots, and the current manifestations of social justice ministry and *praxis*? How are issues of racism, sexism, violence, heterosexism, anti-Semitism, ecological imbalance, and disabilities addressed in practical theology? In some ways, these are the issues that call us back for more, for an encore performance in the world.

FINALE

I have choreographed this book around a predominant theme: theology is the music of religious inquiry. Practical theology is an academic discipline in relation to other theological disciplines. In practical theology, critical reflection is combined with "doing theology": acts of ministering to the poor, the sick, the imprisoned,

19. Ibid.
20. Ibid.

the subjugated, the despairing, the homeless, and the unjustly treated.

Practical theology does not exist in isolation but in orchestration with homileticians, religious educators, spiritual mentors, pastoral care and counseling specialists, liturgists, liberation theologians, missiologists, sociologists, and ethicists. The interconnectedness of the theological disciplines is a motif. Charles Wood writes on the current lack of a comprehensive orientation to theological studies, "It has become very difficult to think of theology as a whole—that is, to think of the collection of studies in a theological curriculum as having any internal unity, or, for that matter, any common aim."[21] In the nineteenth century, universities presented their theology faculties with the collection of studies in a more unified manner often referred to as "theological encyclopedia."[22] Granted, this earlier period was marked by "dogmatic and ecclesiastical control" and less critical thinking.[23] Now our task in theology faculties is to consider how all disciplines may play in concert with one another to create a religious rhythm that honors unity and diversity.

A secondary theme in this book presents all of God's creatures as living instruments. As such, God intends for all persons to enjoy and to be fulfilled in religious inquiry. It is the music of the soul, and we long both to hear it and to participate in the music making. The cases in this book and the role models invite all readers to be involved in reflection–action–*praxis*. We are not acted upon as instruments. Rather, we are the instruments.

This book describes two images to illustrate the interconnectedness of practical theology with other disciplines and areas of inquiry. First, I began with the image of the tree, developed by Friedrich Schleiermacher. It is an organic image with much potential for the necessary discussion in theological education and ministry. To Schleiermacher, the roots, the trunk, the crown with branches all represented various divisions in the nineteenth-century paradigm.

21. Wood, *Vision and Discernment*, v.

22. Farley, "Theology and Practice Outside the Clerical Paradigm," 26.

23. Ibid.

The vital exchange of nurture within the parts of the tree is what I have tried to apply to practical theology-in-relationship. Practical theology students have taken this vital exchange further by pointing out more complicated exchanges within various types of trees. For example, the redwood canopies in coastal California exhibit reversed sap transport or the flow of sap during periods of heavy fog. Fog can be absorbed directly through the redwood leaf canopies, resulting in sap flow in the direction of the soil.[24] Additional studies at the University of Florida have suggested alternate tree root models with lateral roots of a tree extending far beyond what is known as the drip line or circumference of the tree canopy.[25] In a semiarid site in Kenya, the downward flow of sap and water was documented after the first rain at the end of a dry season and after irrigation.[26] In this way, water was distributed to more arid soil.[27] Reflections of the horticultural imagery can then be applied to the flow of ideas and concepts in the field of practical theology. The subfields of the theological curriculum nourish one another. Thus, practical theology nourishes biblical studies, systematic theology, church history, and ethics. In the reverse flow, biblical studies, systematic theology, church history, and ethics nurture practical theology. Always attentive to the surrounding culture of theological inquiry, the life flow of theology moves to the arid areas.

Second, I used the image of musicians-in-relationship, playing their individual instruments but in a way that benefits the whole artistic enterprise. I evoked illustrations of concerts, symphonies, operas, ballets, bands, pop concerts, chamber concerts, songfests, choirs, and chorales. In community, something is created that is larger than the individual parts. In using two images, that of music and that of root-trunk-branches, I emphasize ways that we can be structurally and artistically related to others.

24. Burgess and Dawson, "The Contribution of Fog."

25. Gilman, "Where Are Tree Roots?"

26. Smith, et al. "Reverse Flow of Sap."

27. The students in MN7329, Issues in Practical Theology (Spring 2008), contributed to this discussion. In particular, Doug Wintermute provided the technical data mentioned in the text and Dr. Jim Laughlin added insight.

This book is an overture to practical theology. Practical theology is a spiritual symphony that puts faith in action and action in faith. It offers connectedness not only to other disciplines in theology but to each other. Most of the case studies in the chapters have all had a major element of suffering, from want, injustice, poverty, sexual identity, grief, political injustice. Some of the cases involved an initiative to alleviate suffering, even in the face of a con artist. The following true story of Tiamat's search for an end to her loneliness is another *way of suffering*.

Tiamat's downward movement of grief, anger, despair, and isolation lasted for nearly two years in the parsonage. Tiamat came to the end of her will to live. It was a cold night outside as she paced inside the parsonage on a hill above Lake Union. At midnight she started to walk down the hill toward the wintry water. She would swim out a distance, "then let go, sink down into the darkness and go home to God. The thought was comforting."[28]

At the bottom of the hill, something stood between her and the water's edge. It looked like some kind of barrier made out of sawhorses. Determined on her course of action, Tiamat kept walking. The odd shapes were telescopes she realized as she walked into the midst of the Seattle Astronomy Club! One astronomer in a burst of excitement, thinking she was with the club, asked her to look through his telescope at Jupiter. It really was a beautiful sight, she had to admit. Tiamat confesses, "I couldn't kill myself in the presence of these people who had gotten up in the middle of a cold, spring night, with their home-built Radio Shack telescopes, to look at the stars and planets."[29] The words of a hymn that she had sung in church choir came to her. "The warmth of Samuel Barber's music and the sweetness of James Agee's poetry embraced that moment, held my life in that moment, when I could not hold myself. The poets, the amateur scientists, and the splendid night sky kept me in this world."[30]

28. Brock and Parker, *Proverbs of Ashes*, 114.
29. Ibid.
30. Ibid, 115.

With critical theological reflection, Tiamat realized she had been taught such a life of self-sacrifice that she had become fragmented and isolated from others. She began to claim the continuities and interconnectedness of ordinary life. "The choir and the music filling the sanctuary, the fellowship and activism of the congregation—these sustained me. The ordinary inclination of human beings to share what pleases them, the delight of being awake to the beauty of the night sky, the cool air, the grass beneath my feet—these returned life to my senses. The commonplace translated itself into a deeper knowing. There is a web of connection we live that is greater than sense can tell."[31]

This book is an invitation to connection. It is the connection urged by the psalmists: "Sing joyfully to [God] . . . [play] the harp; make music . . . on the ten-stringed lyre. Sing . . . a new song; play skillfully, and shout for joy" (Ps 33:1–3 NIV). It is to approach the Holy Place where some have stood before us playing instruments (cymbals, harps, and lyres) and some have accompanied on trumpets. After the ark of God's covenant rested in the new temple in Jerusalem on Mount Moriah, the instrumentalists and the singers joined in unison, as with one voice, to give praise and thanks to God.

> Accompanied by musical instruments, they raised their voices as human instruments in praise to [Yahweh] and sang: "[God] is good; [God's] love endures forever." (2 Chr 5:13–14 NIV)

Perhaps this timeless choreography is itself an overture to the purpose of practical theology: love of God, love of neighbor, love of self.

31. Ibid.

Requiem

In a Requiem or Requiem Mass, there are many liturgical forms sung to different melodies and polyphonic settings. Yet the grief is consistent in expression.

In a Requiem, the season of life is the winter of the soul, holding out for hope of resurrection and spring. For some, the Ground of Being holds the roots of what we have constructed in faith. Even in the freezing trauma of loss, when the limbs of love seem amputated, when the trunk has been notched as if by a driver fallen asleep at the wheel, our cold construct stands. It is a cruel way to test the rootedness of our belief system, the tenets of our worldview—the freezing temperatures of trauma, the devastation of drought. In time—if accompanied by hope and support—the pruned branches grow, the winter becomes milder, the rain comes, and the fruits once again drop to the ground.

I have used the image of a tree only as a metaphor in this book. However, I reflect on two persons whose stories reveal the connection and stability they received from contact with an actual tree. One person was Dr. Howard Thurman, civil rights leaders, theologian, philosopher, author, religious leader, and mentor to Dr. Martin Luther King Jr. Dr. Thurman grew up in Daytona Beach, Florida, in a segregated community of blacks. He lost his father at age seven and faced hardships. When he needed strengthening, he had a favorite old oak tree that he sat with and touched for connection. He looked at the stars and the sea and found comfort in nature, especially this old tree.[1] Likewise, author Martha Whitmore Hickman, in her brokenness in the loss of her fourteen-year-old daughter, wrote these words: "In contemplative silence we can sense communion with all people, and with trees, flowers, wind, sky. I remember how, in the anguished months after my daughter died, I would step out into my backyard and commune with the trees—laying my hands against the bark. Sometimes (when I was sure no one was looking!) I put my arms around a favorite tree, and rested against it, as though the common source of life that fed us both would bring me strength and stability."[2] Perhaps in the winter of my life, as the anesthesia of trauma wears off and the reality of absence increases the pain, I too am entering the forest of my faith and holding on for life.

A REQUIEM FOR DAVID, MY SON[3]

To Mom (solo):
I'm sorry I just slipped away the other day
I'm not sick and I'm not in pain
If you need me, just call my name.

I know that I slipped away the other day
So please don't live your life in sadness and tears
God shared me with you for some beautiful years.

I'm sorry I slipped away the other day
Only God knows the reason why
I'll wrap my arms around you when I see you cry.

---

1. Thurman, *Conversations with Howard Thurman.*
2. Whitmore Hickman, *Healing after Loss,* August 7 entry.
3. Written on June 22, 2016, David's 28th birthday.

Requiem

I know that I slipped away the other day
Reflect on our memories and cherish our love
Know that I'll be smiling at you from above

I just slipped away the other day
You didn't know I was here for only a brief stay
Take comfort in the knowing, we'll meet again one bright sunny day.[4]

To David (solo):

I busy myself with order because my life was turned upside down and sideways with your death. I clean out an old file. The receipt for your shoes, Size 12 Vans, is there.

I prepare my IRS tax return. We filed for an extension because of your death.

The bank statements show all the meals we had in Jackson and the trips to Wal-Mart.

I look at my cancelled checks and see your paid dental bill, the electric fence for your dog, Dio.

Where can I hide from you?

I am crying out for you, David.

The phone call about your accident has shaken my life.

When my Call comes, I am ready.

4. Vanessa Sims wrote the section 'To Mom,' for us in January 2015. She has given permission for its use in this book. I wrote the section, 'To David,' as my response. My family is indebted to Vanessa for her creativity and sensitivity to the Spirit of God.

David speaks (solo):

Grieve not. . .

Nor speak of me with tears.

But laugh and talk of me

As though I were beside you.

'Twas heaven here with you . . .

I loved you so.[5]

Mom and David (duet):

Mom: I cannot forget the morgue with your broken body in a black bag, your beautiful strong body. I fell to the floor. I held to the table. The pain. Your shattered body.

David: But Mom, I wasn't there . . . in the body bag.

Mom: I visit the grave. I clean the headstone: David Stevenson Moessner: "Father, Son, Brother, Beloved." I sit close.

David: But, Mom, I am not there.

Mom: Dustin said you died a happy man.

David: I died a very happy man.

Mom: The accident was such a terrible one.

David: Christ was in the car. He carried me gently home.

Relinquishment (divine duet):

Christ: Can you trust him to me?

Mom: No. If I relinquish him, he will be further away from me, from my heart.

Christ: We are one heart.

---

5. This verse adapted from the poem "To Those I Love," Authorship attributed to Isla Paschal Richardson, original source unknown.

Bibliography

Adams Daniels, Geraldine. "Project Rescue—Transportation of a Refugee Family." Unpublished Manuscript. Perkins School of Theology, SMU.

Allen, Diogenes. *Love: Christian Romance, Marriage, Friendship.* Cambridge, MA: Cowley, 1987.

Anderson, Ray S. *The Shape of Practical Theology: Empowering Ministry with Theological Praxis.* Downers Grove, IL: InterVarsity, 2001.

Andrews, Dale P. *Practical Theology for Black Churches: Bridging Black Theology and African American Folk Religion.* Louisville: Westminster John Knox, 2002.

Andrews, Dale P., and Robert London Smith Jr., eds. *Black Practical Theology.* Waco, TX: Baylor University Press, 2015.

Baker-Fletcher, Karen. *Sisters of Dust, Sisters of Spirit: Womanist Wordings on God and Creation.* Minneapolis: Fortress, 1998.

Ballard, Paul, and John Pritchard. *Practical Theology in Action: Christian Thinking in the Service of the Church.* London: SPCK, 1996.

Bennet, John B. *Academic Life: Hospitality, Ethics, and Spirituality.* Bolton, MA: Anker, 2003.

Berling, Judith. *Understanding Other Religious Worlds: A Guide for Interreligious Education.* Faith Meets Faith Series. Maryknoll, NY: Orbis, 2004.

Betz, Hans Dieter, Don Browning, Bernd Janowski, and Eberhard Jungel, eds. *Religion Past and Present: Encyclopedia of Theology and Religion (RGG).* Leiden: Brill, 2007

Boff, Leonardo. *Cry of the Earth, Cry of the Poor.* Translated by Phillip Berryman. Ecology and Justice. Maryknoll, NY: Orbis, 1997.

Bibliography

Bonhoeffer, Dietrich. *The Cost of Discipleship*. Rev. and unabridged. Maryknoll, NY: Orbis Books, 1998.

———. "Who Am I?" *Letters and Papers from Prison*. Edited by Eberhard Bethge. New York: Macmillan, 1967.

Bons-Storm, Riet. *The Incredible Woman: Listening to Women's Silences in Pastoral Care and Counseling*. Nashville: Abingdon, 1996.

Brock, Rita Nakashima, and Rebecca Ann Parker. *Proverbs of Ashes: Violence, Redemptive Suffering, and the Search for What Saves Us*. Boston: Beacon, 2001.

Browning, Don S., ed. *Practical Theology: The Emerging Field in Theology, Church, and World*. San Francisco: Harper & Row, 1983.

———. *A Fundamental Practical Theology: Descriptive and Strategic Proposals*. Minneapolis: Fortress Press, 1991.

Burgess, S. S. O., and T. E. Dawson, "The Contribution of Fog to the Water Relations of Sequoia Sempervirens (D. Don): Foliar Uptake and Prevention of Dehydration." *Plant, Cell and Environment* 27 (2004) 1023–34.

Calahan, Kathleen A., and Gordon S. Mikoski, eds. *Opening the Field of Practical Theology: An Introduction*. Lanham, MD: Rowman & Littlefield, 2014.

Childs, Brian H., and David W. Waanders, eds. *The Treasure of Earthen Vessels: Explorations in Theological Anthropology*. Louisville: Westminster John Knox, 1994. [Festschrift in honor of James N. Lapsley]

Choi, Hee An. *Korean Women and God: Experiencing God in a Multireligious Colonial Context*. Women from the Margins. Maryknoll, NY: Orbis, 2005.

Chopp, Rebecca S. *The Power to Speak: Feminism, Language, and God*. 1992. Reprinted, Eugene, OR: Wipf & Stock, 2002.

Clements, Keith. *Friedrich Schleiermacher: Pioneer of Modern Theology*. Minneapolis: Fortress, 1991.

Cooper-White, Pamela. *The Cry of Tamar: Violence Against Women and the Church's Response*. Minneapolis: Fortress, 2012.

Connaughton, Bernard. "Jeannette Noel, 1916–2006." *The Catholic Worker* 73.4 (2006).

Couture, Pamela D. *Blessed Are the Poor? Women's Poverty, Family Policy, and Practical Theology*. Nashville: Abingdon, 1991.

Couture, Pamela, Robert Mager, Pamela McCarroll, Natalie Wigg-Stevenson, eds. *Complex Identities in a Shifting World: Practical Theological Perspectives*. Zurich: Lit, 2015.

Cozad-Neuger, Christie, ed. *The Arts of Ministry: Feminist-Womanist Approaches*. Louisville: Westminster John Knox, 1996.

Craig, Mary. *Six Modern Martyrs*. New York: Crossroad, 1987.

Dollarhite, Brandon. "Issues in Practical Theology." Unpublished manuscript. Perkins School of Theology, SMU.

Edwards, Kim. *The Memory Keeper's Daughter*. New York: Penguin, 2005.

Farley, Edward. "Practical Theology, Protestant." In *Dictionary of Pastoral Care and Counseling*, edited by Rodney J. Hunter. Nashville: Abingdon, 1990.

Bibliography

———. "Theology and Practice Outside the Clerical Paradigm." In *Practical Theology: The Emerging Field in Theology, Church, and World*, edited by Don S. Browning, 21–41. San Francisco: Harper & Row, 1983.

———. *Theologia: The Fragmentation and Unity of Theological Education.* 1983. Reprinted, Eugene, OR: Wipf & Stock, 2001.

Flanders Dunbar, Helen. "Mental Hygiene and Religious Teaching." *Mental Hygiene* 19 (1995) 353–72.

Friere, Paulo. *Pedagogy of the Oppressed.* Translated by Myra Bergman Ramos. New York: Seabury, 1973.

Gerkin, Charles. *The Living Human Document: Re-envisioning Pastoral Counseling in a Hermeneutical Mode.* Nashville: Abingdon, 1989.

Gilman, Edward F. "Where Are Tree Roots?" Document ENH137, Environmental Horticulture Department, Florida Cooperative Extension Service, Institute of Food and Agricultural Sciences. University of Florida, July 1987.

Graham, Elaine. *Transforming Practice: Practical Theology in an Age of Uncertainty.* 2nd ed. Eugene, OR: Wipf & Stock, 2002.

Graham, Elaine, and Anna Rowlands, eds. *Pathways to the Public Square: Practical Theology in an Age of Pluralism.* Münster: Lit, 2005.

Harris, Joanne. *Holy Fools: A Novel.* New York: HarperCollins, 2004.

Hill Useem, Ruth. "The American Family in India." *Annals of the American Academy of Political and Social Science* 368 (1966) 132–45.

Hiltner, Seward. "Pastoral Care in Europe and America." *Pastoral Psychology* 13 (1962) 10–13.

Holmes, Barbara A. *Joy Unspeakable: Contemplative Practices of the Black Church.* Minneapolis: Fortress, 2004.

Holton, Jan, *Longing for Home: Forced Displacement and Postures of Hospitality.* New Haven: Yale University Press, 2016.

Hornby, Nick. *How to Be Good.* New York: Riverhead, 2001.

Hunter, Rodney, ed. *Dictionary of Pastoral Care and Counseling.* Nashville: Abingdon, 1990.

Hunter, Victor. *Desert Hearts and Healing Fountains: Gaining Pastoral Vocational Clarity.* St. Louis: Chalice, 2004.

Johnson, Suzanne. "Remembering the Poor: Transforming Christian Practice." In *Redemptive Transformation in Practical Theology,* edited by Dana R. Wright and John D. Kuentzel, 189–215. Grand Rapids: Eerdmans, 2004.

Justes, Emma, *Please Don't Tell: What to Do with the Secrets People Share,* Nashville: Abingdon, 2014.

Kwok, Pui-lan. *Postcolonial Imagination and Feminist Theology.* Louisville: Westminster John Knox, 2005.

Lapsley, James N. "Responses, Arguments, Musings, and Further Directions." In *The Treasure of Earthen Vessels: Explorations in Theological Anthropology,* edited by Brian H. Childs and David W. Waanders, 240–62. Louisville: Westminster John Knox, 1994.

Lartey, Emmanuel. *In Living Colour: An Intercultural Approach to Pastoral Care and Counseling.* London: Cassell, 1997.

Marshall, Joretta L. *How Can I Forgive? A Study of Forgiveness.* Nashville: Abingdon, 2005.

McKenzie, Alyce M. *Hear and Be Wise: Becoming a Teacher and Preacher of Wisdom.* Nashville: Abingdon, 2004.

Míguez Bonino, José. *Doing Theology in a Revolutionary Situation.* Philadelphia: Fortress, 1975.

Miles, Rebekah. *The Pastor as Moral Guide.* Minneapolis: Fortress, 1999.

Miller-McLemore, Bonnie. *Also a Mother: Work and Family as Theological Dilemma.* Nashville: Abingdon, 1994.

————. "The Living Human Web: Pastoral Theology at the Turn of the Century." In *Through the Eyes of Women: Insights for Pastoral Care*, ed. Jeanne Stevenson-Moessner, 9–26. Minneapolis: Fortress, 1996.

————, ed. *The Wiley-Blackwell Companion to Practical Theology.* Wiley-Blackwell Companions to Religion. Malden: Wiley-Blackwell, 2012.

Morton, Nelle. *The Journey Is Home.* Boston: Beacon, 1985.

Mudge, Lewis S., and James N. Poling, eds. *Formation and Reflection: The Promise of Practical Theology.* Minneapolis: Fortress, 1987.

Nemirovsky, Irene. *Suite Francaise.* New York: Vintage, 2006.

Niebuhr, H. Richard. *The Purpose of the Church and Its Ministry.* New York: Harper, 1956.

Ogletree, Thomas W. "Dimensions of a Practical Theology: Meaning, Action, Self." In *Practical Theology: The Emerging Field in Theology, Church, and World.* Edited by Don S. Browning. San Francisco: Harper & Row, 1983.

Pak, Su Yon, Unzu Lee, Jung Ha Kim, and Myung Ji Cho, eds. *Singing the Lord's Song in a New Land: Korean American Practices of Faith.* Louisville: Westminster John Knox, 2005.

Parker, Evelyn L., and Anne E. Streaty Wimberly, eds. *In Search of Wisdom: Faith Formation in the Black Church.* Nashville: Abingdon, 2002.

Pauw, Amy Plantinga. "Attending to the Gaps between Beliefs and Practices." In *Practicing Theology: Beliefs and Practices in Christian Life*, edited by Miroslav Volf and Dorothy C. Bass, 33–48. Grand Rapids: Eerdmans, 2002.

Phan, Peter C. *Christianity with an Asian Face: Asian American Theology in the Making.* Maryknoll, NY: Orbis, 2003.

Petrie, Ann, and Jeanette Petrie, producers. "Mother Teresa." VHS. Windsor Home Entertainment, 1986.

Pinkston, John. "What Do You Do When a Stranger Comes into Your Midst?" Unpublished manuscript. Perkins School of Theology, SMU.

Poling, James N., and Donald E. Miller. *Foundations for a Practical Theology of Ministry.* Nashville: Abingdon, 1985.

Procter-Smith, Marjorie. *In Her Own Rite: Constructing Feminist Liturgical Tradition.* Nashville: Abingdon, 1990.

Bibliography

Rieger, Joerg. "Friedrich Schliermacher." In *Empire and the Christian Tradition: New Readings of Classical Theologians*, edited by Kwok Pui-lan, Don H. Compier, and Joerg Reiger. Minneapolis: Fortress, 2007.

Roebben, Bert, and Leo van der Tuin, eds. *Practical Theology and the Interpretation of Crossing Boundaries*. Munster, Ireland: Lit, 2003.

Russell, Letty M. *Household of Freedom: Authority in Feminist Theology*. Philadelphia: Westminster, 1987.

Sayers, Dorothy L. *The Nine Taylors*. New York: Harcourt, Brace & World, 1962.

Schleiermacher, Friedrich. *Christian Caring: Selections from Practical Theology*. Edited by James O. Duke and Howard Stone. Philadelphia: Fortress, 1988.

―――. *Kurze Darstellung des Theologischen Studiums zum Behuf Einleitender Vorlesungen*. Berlin: Realschulbuchhandlung, 1811.

―――. *The Life of Schleiermacher as Unfolded in His Biography and Letters*. 2 vols. Translated by Frederica Rowan. London: Smith, Elder, 1860.

Smith, D. M., N. A. Jackson, J. M. Roberts, and C. K. Ong. "Reverse Flow of Sap in Tree Roots and Downward Siphoning of Water by *Grevillea Robusta*." *Functional Ecology* 13 (1999) 256–64.

Smylie, James. "The Woman's Bible and the Spiritual Crisis." *Soundings* 59 (1976) 305–28.

Stanton, Elizabeth Cady. "The Slave's Appeal." In *Anti-Slavery Depository*. Albany, NY: Weed, Parsons, 1860.

Stanton, Elizabeth Cady et al. *The Woman's Bible, Part I: Comments on Genesis, Exodus, Leviticus, Numbers and Deuteronomy*. New York: European Publishing, 1898.

Stanton, Theodore, and Harriet Stanton Blatch, eds. *Elizabeth Cady Stanton as Revealed in Her Letters, Diary, and Reminiscences*. Vol. 2. New York: Harper, 1922.

Stevenson-Moessner, Jeanne. "Elizabeth Cady Stanton, Reformer to Revolutionary: A Theological Trajectory." *Journal of the American Academy of Religion* 62 (1994) 673–97.

―――, ed. *In Her Own Time: Women and Developmental Issues in Pastoral Care*. Minneapolis: Fortress, 2000.

―――. "A New Pastoral Paradigm and Practice." In *Women in Travail and Transition*, edited by Maxine Glaz and Jeanne Stevenson-Moessner, 200–211. Minneapolis: Fortress, 1991.

―――. *Portable Roots: Transplanting the Bicultural Child*. Newcastle, UK: Cambridge Scholars, 2014.

―――. "The Psychology of Women and Pastoral Care." In *Women in Travail and Transition*, eds. Maxine Glaz and Jeanne Stevenson-Moessner. Minneapolis: Fortress, 1991.

Thurman, Howard. *Conversations with Howard Thurman Hosted by Landrum Bolling*. Video interview. San Francisco: Howard Thurman Educational Trust, 1978.

Bibliography

Tracy, David. "The Foundations of Practical Theology." In *Practical Theology: The Emerging Field in Theology, Church, and World*, edited by Don S. Browning. San Francisco: Harper & Row, 1983.

Viau, Marcel. *Practical Theology: A New Approach*. Boston: Brill, 1998.

Volf, Miroslav, and Dorothy Bass, eds. *Practicing Theology: Beliefs and Practices in Christian Life*. Grand Rapids: Eerdmans, 2002.

Vreeland, Susan. *The Passion of Artemesia*. New York: Penguin, 2002.

Whitfield, Rodney. "A Case of Hospitality." Unpublished manuscript. Perkins School of Theology, SMU.

Whitmore Hickman, Martha. *Healing after Loss: Daily Meditations for Working through Grief*. New York: Avon Books, 1994.

Wood, Charles M. *Vision and Discernment: An Orientation to Theological Study*. 1985. Reprinted, Eugene, OR: Wipf & Stock, 2002.

Wright, Dana R., and John D. Kuentzel, eds. *Redemptive Transformation in Practical Theology*. Grand Rapids: Eerdmans, 2004.

Annotated Bibliography

I. DICTIONARIES AND ENCYCLOPEDIAS

Betz, Hans Dieter et al., eds. *Religion Past and Present: Encyclopedia of Theology and Religion (RGG)*. Leiden: Brill, 2007.

This fourth edition of a prestigious and international resource is an excellent compendium of articles on theology and religion; there is a section on practical theology, and there are connections made between practical theology and other subjects. For example, see Jeanne Stevenson-Moessner, "Bible V. Practical Theology," 2:20. The fourth edition has a more ecumenical approach to practical theology and includes such movements as liberation theology and postcolonialism.

Farley, Edward. "Practical Theology, Protestant." In *Dictionary of Pastoral Care and Counseling*, edited by Rodney J. Hunter. Nashville: Abingdon, 1990.

Farley offers a succinct history of the term *practical theology* with special attention to the eighteenth-century European treatment of practical theology as a "science," a field of inquiry in the university setting. Farley unfolds the European models of practical theology with contemporary correctives. Following a section on persisting issues in the field, Farley concludes with a compact but broad bibliography. Note: A supplement to this dictionary, *Pastoral Care and Counseling: Redefining the Paradigms* (ed. Nancy J. Ramsay [Nashville: Abingdon, 2005]), offers invaluable updates and insights to some of the original material.

II. EDITED VOLUMES[1]

Andrews, Dale P., and Robert London Smith, Jr., eds. *Black Practical Theology* Waco, TX: Baylor University Press, 2015.

The editors of this collection work as practical theologians whose scholarship has been shaped by black church life and black theology. They aim to set up a "trialogue" among practical theologians of various subdisciplines, black constructive, biblical, or ethics theological scholars, and black church leaders or parachurch pastors. The praxis orientation to practical theology engages traditions and historical life but moves with prophetic force into strategies and visions for transformation of worldviews, traditions, and practices.

Browning, Don S., ed. *Practical Theology: The Emerging Field in Theology, Church, and World.* San Francisco: Harper & Row, 1983.

Growing out of conversations with colleagues at the Divinity School of the University of Chicago and flowing into a conference convened by the Divinity School's Institute for the Advanced Study of Religion, practical theology became the subject of theological deliberation. Browning raises numerous questions to probe the issue: "Is it possible that [ministers and lay people] intuitively sense

1. The next sections will include earlier texts that are foundational in the field as well as more contemporary works.

that much of philosophical and systematic theology, although important, is still somehow incomplete, leaving out matters necessary to give theology a cutting edge in the world in which most of us live?" (2). Browning instigates a rigorous foray into the neglected area of practical theology. Edward Farley, John Burkhart, David Tracy, and Thomas Ogletree bring historical and foundational perspectives to the theological table. Dennis McCann, Leander Keck, James Fowler, and James Lapsley serve up their specialties in the areas of social action, rhetoric, spiritual formation, pastoral care, and public policy. David Tracy's presentation of mutual critical correlation between practical theology and the world offers a public theology: "This leads me to propose that practical theology is the mutually critical correlation of the interpreted theory and praxis of the Christian fact and the interpreted theory and praxis of the contemporary situation" (76). Each chapter is deserving of attention; the conversation in these pages marks a historical period in practical theology's renewal in North America.

Calahan, Kathleen A., and Gordon S. Mikoski, eds. *Opening the Field of Practical Theology: An Introduction.* Lanham: Rowman & Littlefield, 2014.

Fifteen practical scholars work to "open" the disciplinary conversations among practical theologians. Instead of offering conceptual models of the field, they offer "approaches" to reflect the open-ended and collaborative character of practical theology. Eleven major concerns integrate and guide the work of these contributors. Among the concerns are the following elements: attentive to theory-practice complexity; teleological and eschatological; oriented to multidimensional dynamics of social context and embodiment; hermeneutical. Emphasis is placed on the plurality of "approaches" in practical theology although mention is made of the interdisciplinary engagement with other theological fields.

Childs, Brian H., and David W. Waanders, eds. *The Treasure of Earthen Vessels: Explorations in Theological Anthropology.*

Louisville: Westminster John Knox Press, 1994. [Festschrift in honor of James N. Lapsley]

Following Schleiermacher's exploratory examination of human experience as a starting point of theological inquiry, Lapsley, according to Waanders, connects "traditional theological perspectives on anthropology while maintaining links to modern approaches in that he has grasped the issues that have been most central in the theological tradition and has reworked them in ways that have integrity within the current context of the human sciences" (4). A major contribution of Lapsley's work is to shift the focus of "salvation" from the past and unhealthy history of the individual to the present and future health of the self. In this collection of essays, former students and colleagues respond to Lapsley's practical theological anthropology.

Couture, Pamela, Robert Mager, Pamela McCarroll, and Natalie Wigg-Stevenson, eds. *Complex Identities in a Shifting World: Practical Theological Perspectives.* Zurich: Lit, 2015.

Growing out of the 2013 conference of the International Academy of Practical Theology at the Toronto School of Theology, Toronto, Ontario, Canada, this collection of essays reflects a world shaped by postmodernism, postcolonialism, indigenous experience, Christian-Muslim dialogue, and the voices of First Nations. The first section focuses on narrativity and identity from various perspectives including those of students in theological education who are preparing for ministry in intercultural settings. The element of "encounter" in addition to narrative and theological reflection becomes essential in this preparation.

Cozad-Neuger, Christie, ed. *The Arts of Ministry: Feminist-Womanist Approaches.* Louisville: Westminster John Knox, 1996.

Drawing from the arenas of theological education that fall under the rubric of practical theology, contributors from pastoral care, preaching and worship, Christian education, administration, ethics, and pastoral counseling use feminist social theory to inter-face with theology and practice in ministry. This transformative approach results in a feminist and womanist practical theology.

Graham, Elaine, and Anna Rowlands, eds. *Pathways to the Public Square: Practical Theology in an Age of Pluralism.* Münster: Lit, 2005.

The theme of the 2003 International Academy of Practical Theology, which met in Manchester, England in 2003, was the relationship between the concerns of practical theology and public theology. The lively theological discourse includes input from Marcel Viau, Duncan Forrester, Friedrich Schweitzer, Riet Bons-Storm, William Storrar, Klaus Wegenast, Daniel Louw, Karl Ernst Nipkow, Esther Reed, and notable others. "Questions, of whether a 'public theology' is possible in a globalizing, secular and pluralist world, and the shape it will take in any particular context, form the central thread to this volume, and elicit a rich and diverse response" (5).

Kelcourse, Felicity, and K. Brynolf Lyon, eds. *Transforming Wisdom: Pastoral Psychotherapy in Theological Perspective.* Eugene, OR: Cascade Books, 2015.

In the field of Practical Theology, pastoral psychotherapists work in the interstices of emotional vulnerability, theological sensibilities, and spirituality. It is these latter two realities with which the volume concerns itself. In the second decade of the twenty-first century, how does the language of faith interact with the practice of therapy? The authors avoid a reductionistic paradigm and lead us into a language of breath, suffering, and joy.

Miller-McLemore, Bonnie, ed., *The Wiley-Blackwell Companion to Practical Theology.* Wiley-Blackwell Companions to Religion. Malden, MA: Wiley-Blackwell, 2012.

This substantial volume reflects the intellectual and institutional growth of the field of practical theology in the last half century.

Miller-McLemore uses the term "practical theology" to refer to four distinct enterprises: a discipline among scholars; an activity of faith; a method for studying theology in practice; a curricular area of subdisciplines in a theological institution. This fourfold definition becomes descriptive rather than prescriptive as 56 authors from varying cultural contexts and educational locations grapple with practical theology's dynamic character.

Mudge, Lewis S., and James N. Poling, eds. *Formation and Reflection: The Promise of Practical Theology.* Minneapolis: Fortress, 1987.

Eight contributors probe both approaches to practical theology: formation and reflection. Emerging from a series of seminars sponsored by the Association of Theological Schools, editors Mudge and Poling seek to close the cleft between theological academics and the shared life of faith (xvi). Contributors Don Browning, Rebecca Chopp, Edward Farley, Thomas Groome, David Tracy, James Whitehead, and Charles Winquist critically address the movement among seminary, university, and divinity school faculty that takes the process of formation of Christian community and personhood as a theme for critical reflection (xiv). Noteworthy in this engaging volume is the editors' brief review of recent literature, largely North American, in the field called practical theology (see editors' introduction, xiv-xvi).

Roebben, Bert, and Leo van der Tuin, eds. *Practical Theology and the Interpretation of Crossing Boundaries.* Münster: Lit, 2003.

This Festschrift in honor of M. P. J. van Knippenberg draws largely from the faculty of theology of Tilburg University. The theme is that of boundary and boundary crossing. For van Knippenberg, practical theology was the field of activity that constituted the boundary area between Christian message and changing situation (11). "The boundary area of practical theology is that which lies between message and praxis, which is challenged by the message and by the praxis in which that message is or is not embraced" (12). Practical theology works in the boundary between the visible and the invisible, the transcendent and the immanent, death and the immortal life. The essays in this volume reflect on the "boundary status of good scholarship in practical theology" (13). An interdisciplinary approach involves many of the practical theology faculty at Tilburg.

Volf, Miroslav, and Dorothy Bass, eds. *Practicing Theology: Beliefs and Practices in Christian Life*. Grand Rapids: Eerdmans, 2002.

The editors and eleven contributors address twelve Christian "practices." Rather than articulating a Christian way of life as a whole, the authors comment on things people do in community over time to respond to human need in light of God's active presence. For example, Amy Plantinga Pauw states, "When belief shapes practice in an excellent way, we celebrate God's grace, not human effort" (48). The essays challenge readers to think more systematically and theologically about the shape and character of these Christian practices. Although the definition of Christian practices may vary from chapter to chapter, all contributors acknowledge the gaps between beliefs and practice. With this volume, the possibilities for narrowing this gap in the Christian life are offered.

Wright, Dana R., and John D. Kuentzel, eds. *Redemptive Transformation in Practical Theology*. Grand Rapids: Eerdmans, 2004.

This *Festschrift* honors the late Dr. James Loder, who highlighted the need for a scientific practical theology, "a practical theological science of Spirit-to-spirit relations" (403). To be relevant in the twenty-first century, practical theology must involve an interplay between "science" and "spirit." To Loder, the "spirit" implied the Holy Spirit as well as human spirit. In this collection of essays, his former students work as "interdisciplinary scientists" (403). For example, Susanne Johnson interfaces global economics, ideologies of power, and revitalizing ethics as practical theology. Daniel S.

Schipani interrelates exegesis, social scientific analysis, and the "logic of transformation" as practical theology (130).

III. MONOGRAPHS

Andrews, Dale P. *Practical Theology for Black Churches: Bridging Black Theology and African American Folk Religion.* Louisville: Westminster John Knox, 2002.

"Practical theology" is a bridge between living in the world and living in a faith community. Andrews addresses this critical connection. Central to the book is his exposure of the chasm between black theology, particularly as located in the academy, and black churches. "This study bridges the theological axioms of black theology and the faith claims operating in African American folk religion" (2).

Browning, Don S. *A Fundamental Practical Theology: Descriptive and Strategic Proposals.* Minneapolis: Fortress, 1991.

In the tradition of practical wisdom (*phronesis*), Don Browning argues that the religious community's tradition is the repository and resource for both memory and wisdom. Using three religious communities as actual cases, Browning illustrates the theological movement from practice to theory to practice. The theological task begins with the community in conversation, often precipitated by a crisis. From the community, theory laden questions arise, which propel the community back to their sacred texts and doctrines to result in reformulated responses. Browning's extensive case material draws from three loci: a liberal upper-middle-class Methodist church in a suburban setting in New England, a conservative middle-class Presbyterian church in a county seat in Ohio, and a Pentecostal church on the South Side of Chicago.

Chopp, Rebecca S. *The Power to Speak: Feminism, Language, and God.* 1992. Reprinted, Eugene, OR: Wipf & Stock, 2002.

Feminist discourse from a position of marginality offers not only multiplicity and otherness in theological language, in God images, and in the reading of religious texts, but it offers emancipatory transformation of the social-symbolic order. This transformation at times occurs with resistance to the established order, even the order of theological education. A feminist hermeneutics of marginality examines both social/symbolic economy and social-symbolic theology. Chopp speaks from the nexus of systematic theology, practical theology, and liberation theology.

Couture, Pamela D. *Blessed Are the Poor? Women's Poverty, Family Policy, and Practical Theology.* Nashville: Abingdon, 1991.

Pamela Couture contributes methodologically to the cross-fertilization of theoretical analysis and theological reflection, particularly in the interface of public policy, social sciences, and religion. Relating the classical theological tradition of John Wesley and Martin Luther to contemporary culture, Couture offers an example of the passion of practical theology: the living juncture of theological narrative and transformative practice.

Farley, Edward. *Theologia: The Fragmentation and Unity of Theological Education.* 1983. Reprinted, Eugene, OR: Wipf & Stock, 2001.

Theological education in North American Protestant settings is under review in this extensive essay. The "division of labor" in theological education has resulted in an isolation of the disciplines and a lack of unity among them. The theological "encyclopedia" model originating in nineteenth-century Germany and later adopted in nineteenth-century North America divided the curriculum into four areas of study: Bible, dogmatics, church history, and practical theology. Farley concluded that the product of seminary is not a theologically educated minister. The theological schools have instead produced a "clerical paradigm," or a model of ministerial practice. Farley says of practical theology in particular: "In current theological schools, practical theology frequently becomes simply a pragmatics of ministry" (20). Farley works towards a concept of *theologia* as a means of reclaiming the goal of theological education. "*Theologia*. . . is a sapiential (existential, personal) and praxis-oriented understanding, and as such it is the way faith rises to self-conscious dealing with the world." *Theologia*, or divinity, involves an objective science and a personal knowledge of God. It is individual cognition of God and "a discipline, a self-conscious scholarly enterprise of understanding" (31). Farley's work is important to the current discussion in this book because he also sought an organic unity in the pursuit and passion of theological education.

Friere, Paulo. *Pedagogy of the Oppressed*. Translated by Myra Bergman Ramos. New York: Seabury, 1973.

As Richard Shaull comments in the foreword, "Paulo Friere incarnates a rediscovery of the humanizing vocation of the intellectual, and demonstrates the power of thought to negate accepted limits and open the way to a new future" (12). Friere had devoted his life to illiterates, especially adults, first in his homeland of Brazil, then in Chile. As he worked in the Two-Thirds world, he developed a pedagogy or practice of teaching that assumed a priori that every person was capable of critical and dialogical encounter with his or her world. Even those such as the illiterate and uneducated who have been ensconced in a "culture of silence" can find a voice in the fray to create a new social order and can find self-awareness as a *subject* of history, not an *object*. This struggle unites theory and *praxis* and takes to task the current educational system.

Graham, Elaine. *Transforming Practice: Practical Theology in an Age of Uncertainty*. 1996. Reprinted, Eugene, OR: Wipf & Stock, 2002.

"What if . . . theologians and educators started to teach their biblical criticism, their historical and systematic theology *contextually*? If all theology were seen as *practical* theology?" (8). The authors begin with a query and set to the three arduous tasks of theological reflection: the induction and nurture of members, which includes formation of character; building and sustaining the community of faith in a particular time and place; and communicating the faith to a wider culture, a culture needing signs of God's activity in the world (10–11). The authors understand theology as process and product. They endeavor to close the divide between systematic theology and practical theology (16). Each chapter closes with an annotated bibliography, which becomes an asset to the reader.

Choi, Hee An. *Korean Women and God: Experiencing God in a Multireligious Colonial Context.* Women from the Margins. Maryknoll, NY: Orbis, 2005.

Korean *minjung* theology is rooted in Korean experiences of culture and life. Choi Hee An looks at one of the central themes in *minjung* theology, that of *han*, or a fundamental feeling of defeat, despair, resignation, injustice, resentment, and hurt, and finds it androcentric. "Most minjung theologians as well as other theologians do not want to talk about women's oppression" (5). Choi Hee An begins with women's experience, especially with their God images, both negative and positive. She illustrates how positive images and attributes of God can reconstruct women's understandings of themselves. Thus, she moves in the analysis from lived experience, to theology, to transformed experience.

Justes, Emma, *Please Don't Tell: What to Do with the Secrets People Share.* Nashville: Abingdon, 2014.

Emma Justes as pastoral and practical theologian offers a foundation for listening to secrets. Her theological framework includes the doctrine of God's grace and the parable of the Prodigal Son who was met with grace. Hospitality, redemption, and renewal are theological themes developed through case studies and reflection.

Míguez Bonino, José. *Doing Theology in a Revolutionary Situation.* Confrontation Books. Philadelphia: Fortress, 1975.

While dean of postgraduate studies at Union Theological Seminary in Buenos Aires, Argentina, José Míguez Bonino wrote a brief overview of Latin American liberation theology. One of the chief contributions was his explanation of transformative practice in the world, or *orthopraxis*. "*Orthopraxis*, rather than orthodoxy, becomes the criterion for theology" (81).

Poling, James N., and Donald E. Miller. *Foundations for a Practical Theology of Ministry.* Nashville: Abingdon, 1985.

Poling and Miller address the concern over the fragmentation or diffusion of practical theology into specializations: preaching, counseling, missions, evangelism, administration, and education. The coauthors offer a unifying image for these specializations: the formation of the community of faith. The method of practical theology is as follows: "description of lived experience; critical awareness of perspectives and interests; correlation of perspectives from culture and the Christian tradition; interpretation of meaning and value; critique of interpretation; guidelines and specific plans for a particular community" (69).

Russell, Letty M. *Household of Freedom: Authority in Feminist Theology.* Philadelphia: Westminster Press, 1987.

As feminist theologians and liberation theologians move from action to reflection, or *praxis* to reflection, questions of power and authority are asked. At the time of Letty Russell's writing, many of the well-known practical theologians were men. She wanted to enlarge the "table" of practical theologians; hers was always a round table with places for new perspectives. In this book, she presents God as Housekeeper of all creation. As Housekeeper, God is attentive to those at the bottom rungs of society. For Letty Russell, that is where practical theology begins.

Schleiermacher, Friedrich. *Christian Caring: Selections from Practical Theology.* Edited by James O. Duke and Howard Stone. Philadelphia: Fortress, 1988.

Friedrich Schleiermacher was often called the "founder of modern theology" and a pioneer in the field of practical theology (7). He was dedicated to the belief that practical theology be well-grounded academically and relevant practically. He was the first to present practical theology as a unified field within theological education. He envisioned practical theology as "Christian caring," or the care of souls. His work on pastoral care, which is included in this volume, portrayed pastoral care as "the care of souls in the narrow sense of the word," thus connecting this subfield to the larger unit of practical theology (9).

————. *Kurze Darstellung des Theologischen Studiums zum Behuf Einleitender Vorlesungen.* Berlin: Realschulbuchhandlung, 1811.

This is the original version of the *Brief Outline of Theology as a Field of Study.* This first edition is important to the imagery of organicity as presented in *Prelude to Practical Theology.* A comparison of this early version of Schleiermacher's work can be compared to the 1830 edition in Terrence N. Tice's English translation of the two. See Schleiermacher's *Brief Outline of Theology as a Field of Study,* translated by Terrence N. Tice (Lewiston, New York: The Edwin Mellen Press, 1990).

Wood, Charles M. *Vision and Discernment: An Orientation to Theological Study.* 1985. Reprinted, Eugene, OR: Wipf & Stock, 2002.

In this text, previously published by Scholars Press in 1985, Charles Wood offers a succinct history of the schematization of theology. He traces the lineage of the "fourfold pattern" of theological education, which divides studies into biblical, dogmatic/systematic, historical, and practical—to the Reformation. He offers invaluable insight into Schleiermacher's "threefold pattern" of theological education: philosophical theology, historical theology, practical theology. "Historical theology" according to Schleiermacher covered both exegetical theology (biblical studies) and dogmatic theology. Chapter 3 elaborates in more detailed fashion Schleiermacher's "three dimensions of theology." The fourfold pattern and the threefold pattern shared the same vision: the furtherance of "church leadership" (10). For Schleiermacher, theology as a positive and practical science did not relax any standards of critical scholarship. Wood moves into a five-dimensional rubric for theological inquiry by adding moral theology (or theological ethics) and by reinserting systematic theology as a discipline in itself and also as a mediator and as a coordinator of the other disciplines (52–54). Wood is clear to move away from the usage of practical theology as a collective or catchall term for pastoral functions such as preaching, administration, pastoral care, and so on. He reestablished its location in the pantheon of theological inquiry. It is both *wissenschaftliche* [scientific] and *habitus*. (See David H. Kelsey, *Between Athens and Berlin: The Theological Education Debate* [Grand Rapids, Mich.: Wm. B. Eerdmans, 1993], 208–20.)

In Wood's more recent book, *Attentive to God: Thinking Theologically in Ministry*, coauthored with Ellen Blue (Nashville: Abingdon, 2008), pastoral character and pastoral practice are presented as mutually formative (v). "Practical theology is that aspect of theological inquiry that attends particularly to the questions of how the Christian witness is best realized in a given context" (19).

IV. IMAGES

Living Human Web—Bonnie Miller McLemore. "The Living Human Web: Pastoral Theology at the Turn of the Century." In *Through the Eyes of Women: Insights for Pastoral Care*, edited by Jeanne Stevenson-Moessner, 9–26. Minneapolis: Fortress Press, 1996.

Bonnie Miller-McLemore builds on the work of John Spencer and Catherine Keller in developing the living human web, which illustrates "the dense, multitudinous, contiguous nature of reality" in contrast to static interpretations of reality (17). A living human web cannot be read like a document. Within the web, those who have not spoken can speak from their cultural location. This three-dimensional image, the web, offers access from those who are on the underside of power and lends itself to a feminist inclusivity.

Bonnie Miller McLemore's imagery appeared in the April 7, 1993, issue of *The Christian Century* under the title, "The Human Web: Reflections on the State of Pastoral Theology." It has appeared recently in Robert Dykstra's *Images of Pastoral Care: Classic Readings* (St. Louis: Chalice, 2005) 40–46.

The Living Human Document—Charles Gerkin. *The Living Human Document: Re-envisioning Pastoral Counseling in a Hermeneutical Mode.* Nashville: Abingdon, 1989.

In *Prelude to Practical Theology*, I have referred to Gerkin's imagery of the person as a "living human document." Gerkin attributes this imagery to his meeting with Anton Boisen: "I was attracted to what he said about the study of 'living human documents' and mental illness as a sickness of the soul analogous to fever in the body" (30). This was a major shift in imagery from the person as an empty vessel into whom learning is poured.

V. SUBDISCIPLINES OF PRACTICAL THEOLOGY

These subdisciplines include preaching or homiletics, womanist studies, feminist studies, liturgics, preaching, ethics, public policy, social justice, religious education, gender studies, spirituality or formation, pastoral care and counseling, human developmental theory, and cross-cultural (or intercultural) studies. The following list is only a sampling of the new directions in the field.

Cooper-White, Pamela. *The Cry of Tamar: Violence Against Women and the Church's Response.* Minneapolis: Fortress, 2012.

This comprehensive resource, a practical theological response to various forms of violence, illustrates the place of justice issues within the field of theology. Expanding the story of Tamar in 2 Samuel 13, Cooper-White analyzes both cultural contributors, if not sources, of violence. Sexual boundary violations include pornography, sexual harassment, rape, battering, clergy sexual abuse, child sexual abuse, and ritualistic abuse.

Holmes, Barbara A. *Joy Unspeakable: Contemplative Practices of the Black Church*. Minneapolis: Fortress, 2004.

Holmes describes "communal contemplative practices in Africana contexts" that have often been hidden from view (vii). Some have been lost to posterity. Holmes asserts, "we will need to begin a creative construction of worship options that restore the contemplative aspects of Africana faith and practice" (186).

Holton, Jan, *Longing for Home: Forced Displacement and Postures of Hospitality*. New Haven: Yale University Press, 2016.

The author convinces the reader about the prevalence and trauma of displacement, particularly forced displacement. Holton successfully engages compelling questions about "home" and "homecoming" which are fundamental issues to our identity. Using four distinct groups (the indigenous tribe of Batwa, refugees and displaced persons in Congo and Sudan, homeless persons within the USA, and American soldiers struggling with PTSD), Holton is most persuasive in presenting displacement as an increasing *common* human dilemma! Thus, she engages the field of practical theology with psychology, and sociology.

Kwok, Pui-lan. *Postcolonial Imagination and Feminist Theology*. Louisville: Westminster John Knox, 2005.

The author uses *postcolonial* to mean "not merely a temporal period or a political transition of power, but also a reading strategy and discursive practice that seek to unmask colonial epistemological frameworks, unravel Eurocentric logics, and interrogate stereotypical cultural representations" (2). This reading strategy is being employed in the field of practical theology as well, as theologians read from the position of the marginalized.

Marshall, Joretta L. *How Can I Forgive? A Study of Forgiveness.* Nashville: Abingdon, 2005.

Marshall draws upon biblical and theological assertions to gain clarity about what forgiveness is. Her three theological assertions are as follows: We are created by God to be in right relationships. Relationships are shattered by individual and corporate injustice, sin, and evil. "God intends justice, reconciliation, and wholeness" (27).

McKenzie, Alyce M. *Hear and Be Wise: Becoming a Teacher and Preacher of Wisdom.* Nashville: Abingdon, 2004.

McKenzie juxtaposes four virtues of the wise life from biblical wisdom literature with competing cultural values of "the good life." She contrasts personal formation in community to the prevailing radical individualism of contemporary culture.

Miles, Rebekah. *The Pastor as Moral Guide.* Creative Pastoral Care and Counseling. Minneapolis: Fortress, 1999.

Ethics can be lodged both in the academic disciplines of practical theology and systematic theology. Of key importance to Miles, however, is the location of ethics in the fullness of caring community. "For Christians, our decisions and character are shaped by faith. We are always both ethicists and theologians, because Christian moral reflection is interwoven with theology . . . We learn to be moral in communities of faith" (4). Our moral character and virtue is dependent on these relationships of faith (125). Thus, ethics becomes a matter of *habitus*, of formation, of wisdom.

Miller-McLemore, Bonnie J. *Also a Mother: Work and Family as Theological Dilemma.* Nashville: Abingdon, 1994.

To work and to love—Miller-McLemore acknowledges the challenges of the Christian ideal of self-sacrificial, motherly love, especially when "the mores of a society . . . [have] selectively divided the burdens and rewards of family and work along gender lines" (20). In addition to cultural analysis and gender studies, Miller-McLemore reexamines Erik Erikson's notion of generativity in the light of newfound wisdom, especially the wisdom of mothers.

Pak, Su Yon, Unzu Lee, Jung Ha Kim, and Myung Ji Cho, eds. *Singing the Lord's Song in a New Land: Korean American Practices of Faith*. Louisville: Westminster John Knox, 2005.

This collaborative effort gives an example of cross-cultural studies in practical theology. Second and subsequent-generation Korean Americans discuss both indigenous practices and "broken" practices in their faith communities. Practices of faith such as singing and ricing ceremonies are revealed.

Parker, Evelyn L., and Anne E. Streaty Wimberly, eds. *In Search of Wisdom: Faith Formation in the Black Church*. Nashville: Abingdon, 2002.

Parker and Streaty Wimberly speak of wisdom formation in this way: "Wisdom is a God-given, communally guided and shared quality of our coming to know, understand, appreciate, and act on what it means to sojourn as Christians amidst life's ambiguities" (17). Drawing deep from biblical, African, African American, and African Caribbean Christian religious traditions, such realities as the intergenerational transmission of wisdom and the art of discernment are a hopeful resource for formation in black churches.

Procter-Smith, Marjorie. *In Her Own Rite: Constructing Feminist Liturgical Tradition*. Nashville: Abingdon, 1990.

Liturgics is a vital subdiscipline of practical theology. In this classic work, Marjorie Procter-Smith explores and recovers a forgotten history, that of women's liturgical history. Language, images, and symbolic systems are examined in relationship to the "historical norm," and a new pastoral norm is offered.

Stevenson-Moessner, Jeanne, ed. *In Her Own Time: Women and Developmental Issues in Pastoral Care.* Minneapolis: Fortress, 2000.

Working as practical theologians, eighteen women insightfully critique prevailing developmental theories and carefully tend to neglected areas of psychological, sociological, and theological inquiry. Stages of the life cycle, rites of passage, theories of psychosocial development, intimate violence, and issues of embodiment are incorporated into new theory-building. The contributors challenge traditional ways of understanding the life spectrum. See also *Women Out of Order*, Eds. Stevenson-Moessner and Teresa Snorton; *Through the Eyes of Women*, Ed. Stevenson-Moessner; *Women in Travail and Transition*, Eds. Stevenson-Moessner and Maxine Glaz.

Author Index

Author Index

Subject Index

adagio, 27, 29, 30
allegro, 27, 28, 30
andante, 27–28, 30
Association of Theological
    Schools, 88

Bonhoeffer, Dietrich, 59, 60,
    63–65

case study, 8, 10, 14, 27, 42
Catholic Worker newspaper, 60, 67
Catholic Worker communities, 66
clerical paradigm, 4, 7, 69n22, 91
Clinical Pastoral Education
    (CPE), xiii, 8, 19
colonial, 32, 33, 49
contemplative silence, 74
crescendo, 28
"cup of cold water," 48–49, 51
Communion of Saints (Sanctorum
    Communio), 63–64

Dies Academicus, xii
dynamic symbolism, 9

exegesis, 19–21, 90

feminist, 4, 8, 10, 20, 60, 61,
    86–87, 91, 94, 97, 98, 100

Great Commission, 15, 16, 18
Good Samaritan paradigm, 38, 39

habitus, 36, 96, 99
han, 93
"hearing into speech," 48
historical theology, ix, 2, 5–6, 95

interstitial culture, 35

largo, 27, 29, 32
living human documents, xi, xiii,
    xiv, 19, 97
living human instruments, xi, xiv,
    59, 68
living human web, xiv, 72, 96

Noel, Jeannette, 59–60, 66–68

organic, ix, xiii, 2–3, 5, 6, 10, 21,
    69 92
orthopraxis, 94

philosophical theology, ix, 2, 5
phronesis, 29, 90
practical theology, ix, x, xi–xv,
    1–3, 5–7, 8, 10, 15, 18,
    19–21, 26, 27, 29, 32, 37, 39,
    42, 43, 45–46, 47, 49, 52–53,
    56, 59–60, 68–72, 83–85, 90,
    92, 95–96, 101
praxis, 18–19, 20, 42, 45, 49, 59,
    60, 62, 65, 66, 68, 69, 84,
    92, 94

Subject Index

Requiem, xiv, 1, 73–74

Schleiermacher, Friedrich, ix, xiv,
   2–7, 10–11, 42, 69
scientific practical theology, 89
self-in-relation, xiv, 10
service-delivery paradigm, 34–35
ship-pal-bun, 55
staccato, 28, 32
Stanton, Elizabeth Cady, 59–63

theologia, 7n12, 91–92

theological education, 14, 23, 69,
   86, 91–92, 95–96
"theological encyclopedia," 69, 91
theology, 1
theology-in-relationship, 1, 2,
   10, 70
trialogue, 84

womanist, 8, 20, 21, 86–87, 97
Woman's Bible, 61n7, 62
Women of Uhuru Park, 59–60,
   65–66